CARDINAL WALTER KASPER

MODERN SPIRITUAL MASTERS SERIES

CARDINAL WALTER KASPER

✝

Spiritual Writings

Selected and Translated with
an Introduction by
PATRICIA C. BELLM
AND
ROBERT A. KRIEG

ORBIS BOOKS
Maryknoll, New York 10545

ORBIS BOOKS
Maryknoll, New York 10545

Fathers and Brothers
MARYKNOLL™

Founded in 1970, Orbis Books endeavors to publish works that enlighten the mind, nourish the spirit, and challenge the conscience. The publishing arm of the Maryknoll Fathers and Brothers, Orbis seeks to explore the global dimensions of the Christian faith and mission, to invite dialogue with diverse cultures and religious traditions, and to serve the cause of reconciliation and peace. The books published reflect the views of their authors and do not represent the official position of the Maryknoll Society. To learn more about Maryknoll and Orbis Books, please visit our website at www.maryknollsociety.org.

Library of Congress Cataloging-in-Publication Data

Names: Kasper, Walter, 1933- author.
Title: Spiritual writings / Cardinal Walter Kasper ; selected and translated
  with an introduction by Patricia C. Bellm and Robert A. Krieg.
Description: Maryknoll : Orbis Books, 2016.
Identifiers: LCCN 2016005472 (print) | LCCN 2016016829 (ebook) | ISBN
  9781626981911 (pbk.) | ISBN 9781608336616 (ebook)
Subjects: LCSH: Catholic Church—Doctrines—20th century.
Classification: LCC BX1751.3 .K3613 2016 (print) | LCC BX1751.3 (ebook) |
DDC
  230/.2—dc23
LC record available at https://lccn.loc.gov/2016005472

Contents

Sources and Acknowledgments

The selections in this book were translated from the original German texts into English by Patricia C. Bellm and Robert A. Krieg. In the bibliographic information below, the names of two publishers have been abbreviated: "HV" means Herder Verlag (Publisher), and "MGV" means Matthias Grünewald Verlag (Publisher). Each German text's date of first publication appears in parentheses at the start of the text itself in its respective chapter; the date of a more recent edition of the German text is usually given in the bibliographic information below. When a German text has appeared in English, its English title and initial date of publication are included below after its German bibliographic information. In choosing texts, the editors have favored Kasper's works that have not appeared in English. In each chapter, the bibliographic information at the end of each text includes the abbreviated reference to the text itself and also the pagination of the German edition. The editors opted to translate from the original German texts for the sake of linguistic consistency. When a text has appeared only in English, this is evident in its bibliographic information. For a complete bibliography of Cardinal Kasper's writings, see www.kardinal-kasper-stiftung.de. This book's biblical citations are from *The Catholic Study Bible*, 2nd ed., edited by Donald Senior, John J. Collins, and Mary Ann Getty (New York: Oxford University Press, 2010).

AGP   "Aspekte gegenwärtiger Pneumatologie," in *Gegenwart des Geistes*, ed. W. Kasper (Freiburg: HV, 1979), 7–22.

ATH   "Autonomie und Theonomie" (1982), in *Theologie und Kirche*, I, ed. W. Kasper (Mainz: MGV, 1987), 145–65. "Autonomy and Theonomy," in *Theology and Church* (New York: Crossroad, 1989).

BAR *Barmherzigkeit* (Freiburg: HV, 2012). *Mercy* (Mahwah, NJ: Paulist Press, 2014).

BJH "Be Joyful in Hope" (2013), in *The Theology of Walter Kasper*, ed. Kristin M. Colberg and Robert A. Krieg (Collegeville, MN: Liturgical Press, 2014), 296–300.

EIG "Einführung in den Glauben" (1972), in *Das Evangelium Jesu Christi*, ed. George Augustin and Klaus Kramer (Freiburg: HV, 2009). *An Introduction to the Christian Faith* (Mahwah, NJ: Paulist Press, 1980).

EUU "Einmaligkeit und Universalität Jesu Christi," *Theologie der Gegenwart*, 17 (1974): 1–11.

EZG "Es ist Zeit, von Gott zu Reden," in *Die Gottesfrage heute*, ed. George Augustin (Freiburg: HV, 2009), 13–31.

FCJ "Foreword," in *Christ Jesus and the Jewish People Today*, ed. Philip A. Cunningham et al. (Grand Rapids, MI: William B. Eerdmans, 2011), x–xviii.

GEH "Geheimnis Mensch" (1973), in *Zukunft aus dem Glauben*, ed. W. Kasper (Mainz: MGV, 1978), 42–56. "The Mystery of Man," in *Faith and the Future* (1982).

GEI *Der Geist macht lebendig* (Freiburg: Informationszentrum Berufe der Kirche, 1982).

GJC *Der Gott Jesu Christi* (Mainz: MGV, 1982). *The God of Jesus Christ* (New York: Crossroad, 1984).

GSG "Gottes Geist sprengt Grenzen, Gottes Geist schafft Zukunft," in *Ich Will Euch Zukunft und Hoffnung Geben*, ed. Central Committee of German Catholics (Paderborn: Bonifacius Druckerei, 1978), 442–54. "The Spirit Acting in the World to Demolish Frontiers and Create the Future," *Lumen Vitae* 34 (1979).

HEI   "Heilige Zeiten, Heilige Orte: Heilige Zeichen in einer weltlich gewordenen Welt," in *Liturgie as Mitte des christlichen Lebens*, ed. George Augustin and Kurt Koch (Freiburg: HV, 2012), 9–26.

HJC   "Die Hoffnung auf die endgültige Ankunft Jesu Christi in Herrlichkeit," *Internationale Katholische Zeitschrift "Communio*," 14 (January 1985): 1–14. "Hope in the Final Coming of Jesus Christ in Glory," *Communio* 12 (Winter 1985).

HTT   "How to do Theology Today" (2013), in *The Theology of Cardinal Walter Kasper*, ed. Kristin M. Colberg and Robert A. Krieg (Collegeville, MN: Liturgical Press, 2014), 248–57.

ISE   "Individual Salvation and Eschatological Consummation," in *Faith and the Future*, ed. John P. Galvin (New York: Paulist Press, 1994), 7–24.

JCG   "Jesus Christus–Gottes endgültiges Wort," *Internationale katholische Zeitschrift Communio* 30 (2001): 18–26. "Jesus Christ: God's Final Word," *Communio* 28 (Spring 2001).

JDC   *Jesus der Christus* (Mainz: MGV, 1974). *Jesus the Christ* (Mahwah, NJ: Paulist Press, 1976).

KAK   *Katholische Kirche* (Freiburg: HV, 2011). *The Catholic Church* (New York: Bloomsbury Academic, 2015).

KAT   *Katholischer Erwachsenen-Katechismus*, ed. German Bishops' Conference (Bonn: Verband der Diözesen Deutschlands, 1985). *The Church's Confession of Faith* (San Francisco: Ignatius Press, 1987).

KUS   "Die Kirche als Universales Sakrament des Heils," in *Glaube im Prozess*, ed. Elmar Klinger and Klaus Wittstadt (Freiburg: HV, 1984), 221–39.

NGC "Neuansätze gegenwärtiger Christologie," *Christologische Schwerpunkte*, ed. W. Kasper (Düsseldorf: Patmos Verlag, 1980), 17–36.

PTE "Paths Taken and Enduring Questions in Jewish–Christian Relations Today," in *The Catholic Church and the Jewish People*, ed. Philip A. Cunningham et al. (New York: Fordham University Press, 2007), 3–11.

RSO "Renewal from the Source: The Interpretation and Reception of the Second Vatican Council" (2013), in *The Theology of Walter Kasper*, ed. Kristin M. Colberg and Robert A. Krieg (Collegeville, MN: Liturgical Press, 2014), 278–95.

TPB "Das theologische Problem des Bösen," in *Teufel, Dämonen, Besessenheit*, ed. Karl Lehmann (Mainz: MGV, 1978), 41–69. "The Theological Problem of Evil," in *Faith and the Future* (1982).

VEW "Vorwort: Einheit–damit die Welt glaubt," in *Wege zur Einheit der Christen*, ed. George Augustin and Klaus Krämer (Freiburg: HV, 2012), 17–34.

WAH "Die Wahrheit in Liebe: Wortlaut der Bischofsansprache am Weihetag," *Katholisches Sonntagsblatt* (#27, 1989): 36f.

WHG *Wo das Herz des Glaubens Schlägt*, with Daniel Deckers (Freiburg: HV, 2008).

WKC "Die weltverwandelnde Kraft der christlichen Liebe," in *Liebe verwandelt die Welt*, ed. Klaus Hemmerle (Mainz: MGV, 1980), 25–52. "The Power of Christian Love to Transform the World," in *Faith and the Future* (1982).

ZDF "Die Zukunft der Frömmigkeit," in *Zukunft aus dem Glauben*, ed. W. Kasper (Mainz: MGV, 1978), 66–70.

"The Future of Devotion to God," in *Faith and the Future* (1982).

ZUG "Die Zukunft aus dem Glauben," in *Zukunft aus dem Glauben*, ed. W. Kasper (Mainz: MGV, 1978), 9–41. "The Future and Faith," in *Faith and the Future* (1982).

ZVH "Die Zusage von Heil" in *Die Zukunft des Menschen*, ed. Ludger Honnefelder and Matthias C. Schmitt (Paderborn: Ferdinand Schöningh Verlag, 2007), 87–104.

***

This book's editors, Patricia C. Bellm and Robert A. Krieg, wish to acknowledge some of the people who made this book possible. George Augustin, S.A.C., Stefan Laurs and Ingo Proft of the Kardinal-Walter-Kasper-Institut (Vallendar, Germany) provided energetic assistance in obtaining permissions. John R. Betz offered invaluable advice regarding some translations into English. Kristin M. Colberg and Katherine F. Elliot offered constructive criticisms of the Introduction.

Robert Krieg is grateful to his long-standing mentors in German Catholic theology: Michael A. Fahey, S.J, Francis Schüssler Fiorenza, Josef Meyer zu Schlochtern, Thomas F. O'Meara, O.P., and Hermann J. Pottmeyer. Also, he is thankful, once again, for the support and astute counsel of his spouse Elizabeth Fee Krieg.

Patricia Bellm is grateful for the encouragement and wisdom of her spouse Harald and her adult children Annalena, Sebastian, and Charlotte.

The editors deeply appreciate the expert work of Robert Ellsberg and the editorial team of Orbis Books.

Finally, Patricia Bellm and Robert Krieg owe a debt of gratitude to Cardinal Walter Kasper for his spiritual–theological writings. They personally benefitted as they translated his rich texts into English. Further, they are grateful to the cardinal for his comments on a draft of this book and for his gracious Foreword.

Chronology

1933–1952   Born on March 5, in Heidenheim an der Brenz. Moves with his parents to Wäschenbeuren. His two siblings are Hildegard and Inge. In 1946, moves with his parents and sisters to Wangen in the Allgäu Alps.

1952–1958   Studies philosophy and Catholic theology at the University of Tübingen and resides at the Wilhelmstift Seminary. Ordained a priest for the Diocese of Rottenburg–Stuttgart on April 6, 1957. Engages in full-time pastoral ministry for one year in Stuttgart.

1958–1964   Undertakes graduate studies in theology at the University of Tübingen. Completes his doctoral dissertation in 1961, published in 1962: *Die Lehre von der Tradition in der Römischen Schule* (The Doctrine of Tradition in the Roman School). Completes his Habilitation in 1964, published in 1965: *Das Absolute in der Geschichte: Philosophie und Theologie Geschichte in der Spätphilosophie Schellings* (The Absolute in History: The Philosophy and Theology of History in the Late Philosophy of Schelling).

1964–1970   Professor of dogmatic theology at the University of Münster. Appointed by the German bishops to participate in the International Lutheran–Catholic Dialogue. Publications include in 1965, *Dogma unter dem Wort Gottes*; in 1967, *The Methods of Dogmatic Theology*.

1970–1989   Professor of dogmatic theology at the University of
             Tübingen. Publications include in 1972, *An Intro-
             duction to the Christian Faith*; in 1974, *Jesus the
             Christ*; in 1977, *Theology of Marriage*; in 1982,
             The God of Jesus Christ; in 1985, *The Church's
             Confession of Faith*. Appointed by John Paul II
             as the theological secretary for the Extraordinary
             Synod of Bishops (October 1985).

1989–1999   Ordained the bishop of Rottenburg–Stuttgart on
             June 17, 1989. President of the German Bishops'
             Commission on the World Church, 1991–99. Co-
             chair of the International Commission for Luther-
             an–Catholic Dialogue, 1994–99. Signs the "Joint
             Agreement on the Doctrine of Justification" in
             Augsburg on October 31, 1999. General editor,
             Lexikon für Theologie und Kirche, 3rd ed., 1993–
             2001.

1999–2010   Moves to Rome and becomes the secretary at the
             Pontifical Council for Promoting Christian Uni-
             ty and also at the Commission for Religious Re-
             lations with the Jews. Named a cardinal by Pope
             John Paul II on February 21, 2001, and becomes
             the president of the Pontifical Council and the
             chair of the commission. Publishes in 2008 *Wo das
             Herz des Glaubens Schlägt* (Where the Heart of
             Faith Beats).

2010–   Retires from his ecclesiastical offices on July 1,
             2010. Publications include in 2011, *The Catholic
             Church*; in 2012, *Mercy*; in 2014, *The Gospel of
             the Family*; in 2015, *Pope Francis' Revolution of
             Tenderness and Love*.

Foreword

In a few months I anticipate recalling with gratitude my sixty years of priestly ministry. The desire to become a priest was placed in my heart at an early age. At the time of my ordination as a priest in 1957, I dedicated this desire for priestly ministry thus: "not that we lord it over your faith, but are workers with you for your joy" (2 Cor 1:24).

My priestly ministry soon took the path into academic theology. This path led me later to the office of bishop and eventually to Rome in the service of the world church and the unity of all Christians. At the time of my ordination as a bishop in 1989, I dedicated my episcopal ministry to: "truth in love" (Eph 4:15).

Thus, ministry for the "Joy of the Gospel" has accompanied me every step of the way. For this reason, along with my strictly theological publications, numerous spiritual texts have come about over the years from my sermons and meditations. In this time of so many significant changes, these writings are meant to contribute "to giving an account of the hope that is in us" (1 Peter 3:15).

Faith in Jesus Christ is a gift to be passed on. Therefore, I owe great gratitude to Patricia C. Bellm and Robert A. Krieg for taking the trouble to select some of the texts written since 1972 and for making them accessible in English to a wider public. I hope that this gift for the jubilee of my priesthood will become a gift for as many readers as possible.

Walter Cardinal Kasper
Rome, Pentecost 2016

Introduction

"Joyful in Hope"

Cardinal Walter Kasper, along with 114 other cardinals, moved into the Vatican's guesthouse, Casa Santa Marta, on Tuesday, March 12, 2013, for the conclave that would elect a successor to Pope Benedict XVI. Since the cardinal had just received copies of his book *Misericordia*, the Spanish edition of his *Barmherzigkeit* (2012), he brought a few of them with him. In 2014, the book appeared in English entitled *Mercy*.

After unpacking his bag in his assigned room, Kasper walked across the hall and gave a copy of *Misericordia* to the Archbishop of Buenos Aires, Cardinal Jorge Mario Bergoglio, S.J. On March 13, Cardinal Bergoglio was elected pope, choosing the name Francis.

Everything happened quickly. Cardinal Kasper did not know whether Cardinal Bergoglio/Pope Francis had even glanced at *Misericordia*. On March 17, he watched on television as Pope Francis prayed the Angelus at noon and then offered some comments. In particular, the new pope praised *Misericordia* and its author: Cardinal Kasper is "a superb theologian, a fine theologian" whose book on mercy "has done me a lot of good."

Three days earlier, Kasper had lauded Pope Francis in an interview with the newspaper *Schäbische Zeitung*: "Cardinal Bergoglio was my candidate from the start; from the beginning of the conclave, I voted for him. He represents a new beginning in the church, for a humble and fraternal church which is there for all people, a church which returns to its wellspring, the Gospel."

Cardinal Kasper, who had turned eighty on March 5, 2013, assumed that, after the papal election, he would remain in "retirement," writing articles and books. However, he soon learned that Pope Francis was not finished with his surprises. In late 2013, the pope approached the cardinal with two requests. He asked Kasper to give a major address on the family to the Council of Cardinals on February 20, 2014. This address has since appeared entitled *The Gospel of the Family*. Further, Francis invited Kasper to contribute to the Synod of Bishops on the family in October 2014 and again in October 2015.

Pope Francis surely has high regard for Kasper and his theology. It is timely therefore to address three questions. First, who is Walter Kasper, and what is his life story? Second, what is the coherence of Kasper's life and theology? Third, what is the best access to Kasper's spiritual-theological writings?

CARDINAL KASPER'S LIFE JOURNEY

In 2008, on the occasion of his seventy-fifth birthday, Kasper published his memoir entitled "Where the Heart of Faith Beats" (*Wo das Herz des Glaubens Schlägt* [WHG]). (The bibliographic references throughout this introduction are to WHG, unless otherwise noted.) In his memoir, the cardinal explains that the book's title refers to the vibrant faith of the people he met as bishop of Rottenburg–Stuttgart. In these encounters with people throughout Germany and also around the world, he was inspired and guided by people's "heart of faith." He writes, "I have been able to participate a bit in the *joys and sufferings* of the church in the world. Here and there, our dioceses and the church in Germany were permitted to help bring *hope and light* into the world. I am grateful to have experienced where and how the *heart of faith* beats" (p. 126; our italics).

Kasper's statement is significant for it manifests his threefold commitment to the "*heart of faith,*" to "*hope and light,*" and to people's "*joys and sufferings.*" In other words, it expresses the cardinal's dedication to faith, hope, and love (1 Cor 13:13).

Moreover, Kasper's statement implies his devotion to that which is the Source and Goal of the three theological virtues: the God who is the Father and the Son and the Holy Spirit (Mt 28:19). Who is this man in pursuit of faith, hope, and love? Kasper's identity emerges as we recall his life's five phases: 1933–57, student, seminarian, and priest; 1957–89, priest and professor; 1989–98, bishop of Rottenburg–Stuttgart; 1999–2010, Vatican official and cardinal; 2010–present, papal advisor.

1933–1957, Student, Seminarian, and Priest

Walter Kasper was born on March 5, 1933, in Swabia (southwest Germany), specifically in Heidenheim on the Brenz River, not far from Stuttgart. On this same day, Adolf Hitler secured his power as the nation's chancellor when the National Socialist (Nazi) Party won a plurality of seats in the Reichstag, the Weimar Republic's legislative assembly. Kasper's parents—Franz Josef (b. 1901) and Theresia (b. 1902)—rejoiced at their son's birth, but they were troubled by Hitler's "election." Frau Kasper subsequently quipped that her firstborn had spared her from a political confrontation: if she had gone to the polls instead of giving birth to Walter, she would have voted against Nazi candidates; her negative vote would have likely become known to Heidenheim's Nazis.

Over the next five years, Herr Kasper—a school teacher and church organist—and Frau Kasper welcomed into their family Walter's sisters Hildegard and then Inge. During these years, they moved from Heidenheim to Wäschenbeuren, outside of Stuttgart. Although Herr Kasper with Frau Kasper opposed Hitler's National Socialism, he had little choice when in late 1939 he was conscripted into the Wehrmacht's civil defense. He was called to military duty because Hitler's invasion of Poland on September 1 had ignited World War II.

For the next six years, Herr Kasper was allowed only occasional, brief visits with Frau Kasper and their three children. He became a prisoner-of-war in north Germany in the spring

of 1945. Released in late December, he made his way south to
Wäschenbeuren, not knowing the fate of his family. Nor did Frau
Kasper know whether her husband had survived the war's end.
On January 1, 1946, Herr Kasper walked into their home, which
had been partially destroyed by Allied bombs. Amazingly, Herr
Kasper had not been injured or killed during the last months of
the war, and Frau Kasper with Walter, Hildegard, and Inge had
survived the bombing of their village.

Herr and Frau Kasper then packed their belongings and relo-
cated to a house in Herr Kasper's village-of-origin Wangen in
the Allgäu Alps. Today, this residence is the home of Cardinal
Kasper's sister Inge and her husband Roman, who have expanded
it to include accommodations for Walter and Hildegard.

Having survived Hitler's tyranny for twelve years and war for
six of those years, the Kasper family—along with all German
citizens—endured food and fuel shortages until the early 1950s.
Further, they welcomed into their home extended family and
other refugees. During these years, one million Germans died
from malnutrition, typhus, and inadequate heat in the winters,
the coldest of the twentieth century. Not surprisingly, Walter
Kasper has not forgotten the hard times that marked his first
seventeen years: "Today, I can still hear Hitler's voice—a terrify-
ing, hate-filled voice" (p. 16).

Kasper has not allowed, however, the darkness of Nazism to
block the light that radiated from his family and church during
his earliest years:

> There were the good and protected years in a small vil-
> lage on the Ostalb in the circle of our family, which soon
> included my two sisters Hildegard and Inge, two years
> and five years younger than me. Of course, we learned
> at home the fundamentals of the faith and the Chris-
> tian prayers. It was taken for granted that we would
> pray together in the morning and at night, go to church
> together on Sundays and also on many weekdays and

> *on Sunday afternoons for our religious devotions. All of*
> *this occurred without complaints; it was simply beauti-*
> *ful. (p. 12)*

Walter Kasper's family and local church were the mainstays of his formative years. Concerning the former, he writes, "That the family is the seminal unit of society is not an abstract claim for me. In 1945, the family was the only institution which remained and on which one could rely. There were above all the women who during the war and immediately after it directed and maintained daily life while the men were in the war or prison camps" (p. 18). Concerning the church, Kasper recalls not only the church devotions and worship but also the religious processions and pilgrimages:

> *It was especially beautiful in the winter. At night, the*
> *familiar songs of Advent and Christmas were sung in*
> *our family, and, when we were older, accompanied by*
> *our playing the violin and piano. . . . May devotions*
> *were truly important and above all beautiful, to which*
> *one gladly went. During Advent, there were the Rorate*
> *Masses in candle light. . . . There were the frequent pil-*
> *grimages to the Rechberg and sometimes to the Mar-*
> *ian pilgrimage site Schönenberg and also to the grave of*
> *Father Philipp Jeningen, one of the truly holy missionar-*
> *ies of the 17th century. (pp. 21–22)*

At an early age, Kasper became aware of his vocation to the priesthood. He writes, "I cannot remember a specific event that brought this thought to mind; it was not set before me or imposed on me by others such as my parents. It came to me at an age when, in childhood fantasies, someone would like to become many different things. It was in a sense placed in my soul" (p. 22). At school, Kasper excelled in his humanistic studies, including the study of Latin. Through the local church, he participated after the war in the Catholic youth movement, *Neudeutschland*, with its religious celebrations, retreats, camping trips, study groups, and outreach to the poor. There was an occasion when he met the Diocese of Rottenburg–Stuttgart's heroic Bishop Johannes Baptist Sproll (d. 1949) who had condemned Nazism from the pulpit during the 1920s and 1930s and had to flee for his life in 1938. Kasper also came to know Sproll's successor Bishop Carl Joseph Leiprecht (d. 1975). Moreover, in the spring of 1952, at the age of nineteen, Kasper traveled with some members of *Neudeutschland* to Rome where he attended a private audience with Pope Pius XII.

After his graduation from the Gymnasium (high school), Kasper undertook studies in philosophy and theology at the University of Tübingen and lived in Tübingen's Wilhelmstift, the diocesan residence for seminarians. In his studies, he immersed himself in the writings of the Catholic Tübingen School, which had begun in 1817 with the work of Johann Sebastian Drey (d. 1853) and Johann Adam Möhler (d. 1838). This school's three defining traits, which Kasper himself deliberately adopted and still embraces, are "scholarship, participation in the church, and an orientation to praxis" (p. 31). The Catholic Tübingen School, which has shared a building with Tübingen's Protestant theologians for two hundred years, has possessed an ecumenical orientation since its inception. Moreover, in the Wilhelmstift's seminary community, Kasper developed his spiritual life:

> *Every morning began with the church's Liturgy of the Hours, meditation and the celebration of Mass. At night, there was Compline. On Sundays and feast days, a celebratory choir [sang] in the Johannes Church, including Vespers. The rector and spiritual director regularly gave lectures on spirituality, and there were regular days of reflection and annual retreats, of which the talks by Karl Rahner have especially remained with me. (p. 36)*

Walter Kasper was ordained a priest by Bishop Leiprecht in the Rottenburg Cathedral on April 7, 1957. As he explains,

Kasper sees his priesthood as God's action or calling to which he has sought to remain faithful. Ordination "was for me, my parents and my sisters a most blessed day. Not only was my early wish now fulfilled; ordination to the priesthood is a gift and a responsibility. I dedicated myself to the words in 2 Corinthians 1:24: 'Not that we lord it over your faith; rather, *we work together for your joy*, for you stand firm in the faith'" (pp. 38–39; our italics). Following his ordination, Kasper worked for one year in full-time pastoral ministry in Stuttgart's Church of the Heart of Jesus.

1957–1989, Priest and Professor

The social and ecclesial contexts in which Walter Kasper lived from 1957 into 1989 were much different from the world of his formative years. In the early 1950s, West Germany emerged from the ruins of the Third Reich and World War II, and soon became Europe's economic locomotive. In particular, Stuttgart and its surrounding region established itself as an international center for industry and technology. Yet, during the four decades of the Cold War, West Germans anguished as they glimpsed the plight of their relatives and friends in East Germany, especially after the building of the Berlin Wall in August 1961. But, to their's and the world's wonderment, East Germans breached the Wall on November 9, 1989. Chancellor Helmut Kohl immediately initiated the reunification of West Germany and East Germany.

During the postwar years, the Catholic Church too experienced a profound change. During the first half of the twentieth century, the church was predominantly shaped by Baroque Catholicism, that is, by the form of Catholicism from the seventeenth century that accentuates the transcendent God to whom faithful people relate through private prayer, even during Mass. In Baroque Catholicism, priority is given to the Rosary and religious devotions, such as the prayer to the Sacred Heart of Jesus, which was initiated by St. John Eudes (d. 1680) and

St. Mary Margaret Alacoque (d. 1690). This emphasis on personal piety includes, too, the writings of the mystics such as St. Teresa of Avila (d. 1582), St. John of the Cross (d. 1591), and St. Thérèse of Lisieux (d. 1887). Emerging during the Counter-Reformation, Baroque Catholicism defines itself in opposition to Protestantism.

Baroque Catholicism became increasingly problematic during the late 1800s, and by the mid-1900s it was, as Kasper notes, "stifling." Most Catholics and non-Catholics, as well, had the highest esteem for Pius XII during his papacy, but some—including Kasper—saw looming difficulties. Kasper observes that upon Pius XII's death in 1958, it was as though a dike had burst: "The last years of his pontificate were shaped to a certain degree by rigidity. Suddenly the suppressed issues, which had been discussed only in the smallest circles, broke into the open in the community of Tübingen's young scholars" (p. 41).

After Pius XII's death, the unexpected occurred. Milan's Cardinal Angelo Giuseppe Roncalli was elected Pope John XXIII on October 28, 1958. Manifesting an openness to the contemporary world, the seventy-seven-year-old pope announced on January 25, 1959, that he intended to hold an ecumenical council. As a result, John XXIII (d. 1963) opened the Second Vatican Council on October 11, 1962, and his successor Paul VI (d. 1978) adjourned the council on December 8, 1965. Along with the overwhelming majority of bishops at Vatican II, John XXIII and Paul VI welcomed a new form of Catholicism. This Catholicism accentuates that God encounters us within the church—the *communio*, as identified by Kasper—and also outside it as this community of disciples deliberately serves people who are poor, disabled, outcast, and disenfranchised. In this regard, the church emulates the witness of people such as Mother Teresa of Calcutta (d. 1997) and Archbishop Oscar Romero (d. 1980). Further, it undertakes an updated evangelization that includes the World Youth Day, initiated by Pope John Paul II in 1985. Also, Vatican II's Catholicism—as stressed by Popes John XXIII, Paul

VI, John Paul I, John Paul II, Benedict XVI, and now Francis—embraces ecumenism, Jewish–Christian dialogue and constructive interactions with people of other religions and world views. From the outset, the youthful priest and budding theologian Walter Kasper enthusiastically—though not uncritically—endorsed Vatican II's form of Catholicism. He writes,

> *On the one hand, the council was for me the fulfillment of many wishes which had been in me for a long time. Afterwards, the council's documents presented the direction for my entire, further maturation as a theologian. During the council, I was in Rome only once, and I was brought into the council hall by Bishop Leiprecht's secretary Eberhard Mühlbacher who was active in the hall as an usher. Thus, I could observe at least on one occasion the great event throughout a morning. . . . [Vatican II] did not throw the tradition overboard but placed it in a new light and thus opened new perspectives whose potentialities we have not yet brought out. In this sense, the council is the foundation for and the starting point of a new epoch in church history and the Magna Charta for the way of the church in the new century. (pp. 53, 56)*

During the preparations for Vatican II and the council itself, Kasper devoted himself to his studies in theology at the University of Tübingen. Working with Josef Rupert Geiselmann (d. 1970), he wrote his doctoral dissertation on the understanding of tradition as held by the theologians at Rome's Gregorian University and also by the theologians of the Catholic Tübingen School. After completing this scholarly monograph, entitled "The Doctrine of Tradition in the Roman School" (1961), Kasper immediately pursued his Habilitation, the second dissertation required for a faculty position in a German university. He consulted with the French theologian Yves Congar (d. 1995) who was instrumental in bringing about and shaping Vatican II.

The Dominican scholar advised Kasper to study modern philosophy by writing his Habilitation on the later thought of Friedrich Schelling (d. 1854). Acting on Congar's advice and receiving guidance from the theologian Leo Scheffczyk (d. 2005), Kasper wrote "The Philosophy and Theology of History in the Late Philosophy of Schelling" (1964).

In the autumn of 1964, as Kasper was finishing his Habilitation, he joined the faculty of Catholic theology at the University of Münster. Here, he flourished as he taught beside creative scholars such as Johannes Metz, Karl Rahner, S.J. (d. 1984), and Joseph Ratzinger who fifty years later became Pope Benedict XVI. However, in 1970, Kasper bid farewell to his colleagues at Münster and joined the faculty of Catholic theology at the University of Tübingen, where he remained until the summer of 1989. At both universities, Kasper taught lecture courses each semester that attracted several hundred students whose examinations at the end of each semester Kasper read and assessed. At the same time, he held seminars for doctoral students, subsequently directing many of their dissertations. Residing in Tübingen, he regularly visited his parents in Wangen. With his sisters, he was present to his parents as they were dying: his mother in 1981 and his father in 1987. His sister Inge died in 2016.

While in Münster and Tübingen, Kasper published internationally respected works in theology. These include Kasper's *An Introduction to the Christian Faith* (1972), *Jesus the Christ* (1974), *Theology of Marriage* (1977), and *The God of Jesus Christ* (1982). During these years, too, he served as the editor of Tübingen's *Theologische Quartalschrift* and the general editor of the *Lexikon für Theologie und Kirche*. In the early 1980s, Kasper was the primary author—at the invitation of the German bishops—of the Conference of German Bishops' "Catholic Adult Catechism," the *Katholischer Erwachsenen-Katechismus* (1985), available in English as *The Church's Confession of Faith* (1987). In October 1985, at the request of Pope John Paul II, Kasper served as the theological secretary for the Extraordinary

Synod of Bishops in Rome. In this capacity, he developed the widely respected insight that the Second Vatican Council and its documents manifest the ecclesiology of *communio*.

During his twenty-five years as a professor (1964–89), Kasper developed a theology that is congruent with the Catholic Tübingen School's emphasis on (1) scholarship, especially in historical research and biblical studies; (2) participation in the church with its "living tradition"; and (3) praxis, that is, engagement in the church's mission. In doing so, he emphasizes history and culture in contrast to Karl Rahner's transcendental Thomism. Further, he highlights the vitality in the church's tradition, thereby differing from Hans Küng's critique of church tradition. Also, he acknowledges the authority of the local churches, thus taking issue with the focus of Joseph Ratzinger/Benedict XVI on the centralized authority of the papacy. Regarding his theological orientation, Kasper writes,

> *I like to pass not as a liberal but as a radical and even more as an open-minded theologian. For "radical" does not mean "fanatical." "Radical" means going back to the radices, to the roots. Only a tree with deep roots can withstand the storm. Only by going back to the origins can we go ahead. Going back to the roots and the sources means leaving stagnant waters and drawing fresh water from the spring. All reforms within church history started from such a turning back to the apostolic origins. In this sense conservative and progressive are not contradictory but complementary. (HTT, 249)*

1989–1998, Bishop of Rottenburg–Stuttgart

As a theologian in Tübingen, Walter Kasper was invited by the bishop of the Diocese of Rottenburg–Stuttgart, Carl Joseph Leiprecht, and his successor Bishop Georg Moser to offer his counsel on issues facing the church. At the time of Kasper's ordination in 1957, Bishop Leiprecht had affirmed Kasper's vocation to become a theologian in the service of the church. Subsequently, Kasper demonstrated this theological orientation in his books, articles, and public lectures. After Bishop Moser's death in 1988, the Diocese of Rottenburg–Stuttgart's Episcopal Electors chose Walter Kasper to be their candidate to succeed Moser. Their choice was affirmed by Pope John Paul II, and Kasper was consecrated bishop in the Rottenburg Cathedral on June 17, 1989. At that time, he dedicated his episcopal ministry to Ephesians 4:15, "living the *truth in love*, we should grow in every way into him who is the head, Christ" (our italics). With this dedication as his pole star, Kasper led the Diocese of Rottenburg–Stuttgart from 1989 to 1999 and subsequently served as the Vatican's leader for ecumenism and Jewish relations from mid-1999 to mid-2010.

The developments in the world and the church from 1989 to 2010 set the backdrop of Kasper's episcopal leadership. The Soviet Union's implosion and the subsequent abrupt economic, political, and social changes in East Germany and Eastern Europe led to the influx of thousands of refugees into the former West Germany. At the same time, the gap between the world's rich and poor widened into a vast chasm, and the crisis of the Palestinian people, the Middle East's social and political instability, and the rise of terrorism disrupted the international community. During these years, Pope John Paul II (d. 2005) and his successor Pope Benedict XVI initiated doctrinal directives and institutional and liturgical instructions aimed at strengthening the church's identity amid society's increasing secularism, moral relativism, and religious indifference. This "restoration" was welcomed by some Catholics, but it alienated others who saw it eclipsing the church's mission and relevance to the contemporary world. Beginning in 2002, the church itself entered into a crisis with the media's disclosures of the priest sex-abuse scandals—disclosures that started in North America and soon entered the public domain in Europe and the other continents as well. These revelations eroded the credibility of priests, bishops,

and Vatican officials, and they exposed blind spots in the pontificate of John Paul II.

When Walter Kasper assumed the episcopal leadership of
Germany's fourth largest diocese in June 1989, he immediately
faced complicated issues: the decline in church participation, the
breakdown of marriage and family, the moral malaise among
youth, the sharp rise in the number of senior citizens, and the
plight of the immigrants and refugees streaming into Germany.
As he addressed these dilemmas, Bishop Kasper sought to learn
from the diocese's laity and priests. He visited a different parish
every weekend, presiding and preaching at all Masses. Also, he
held synods and other assemblies, for example, of young people
and married couples. Further, at the request of the German Bishops' Conference, Kasper assumed leadership of the conference's
"World-Church Commission." In this position, he was required
to travel to Africa, Asia, and Latin America in order to oversee
German Catholics' generous contributions to Catholic dioceses
and institutions around the world, and also to international
humanitarian agencies.

At the same time, Bishop Kasper remained active in ecumenism, for example, participating in the "Faith and Order
Commission" of the World Council of Churches. Also, having
served since 1964 as a representative of the German bishops in
the Lutheran–Catholic dialogue, he became in 1994 the cochair
of the International Lutheran–Catholic Commission. As such,
Kasper and Lutheran Bishop Christian Krause guided the dialogue so that it bore fruit in the Joint Agreement on the Doctrine
of Justification, which Kasper and Krause signed at St. Anna's
Church in Augsburg on October 31, 1999.

In the course of his meetings with the laity and priests of the
Diocese of Rottenburg–Stuttgart, Kasper became acutely aware
of the canonical impasse for divorced Catholics who had remarried without receiving an annulment of their first marriages. He
began to look for a path forward for these people. During 1992
and 1993, building on a 1972 publication by Joseph Ratzinger,

Kasper collaborated with Bishops Karl Lehmann of Mainz and Oskar Saier of Freiburg im Breisgau in designing a pastoral process—separate from an annulment—by which divorced and remarried Catholics could receive the sacraments. Before implementing this noncanonical alternative, the three bishops proposed it to Cardinal Joseph Ratzinger, the Prefect of the the Doctrine of the Faith (CDF). They subsequently met in Rome on three occasions with Ratzinger and the CDF. At the third meeting in 1994, they were directed by Cardinal Ratzinger not to proceed with their pastoral instruction. Although they disagreed with Ratzinger's directive, they complied with it. Twenty years later, Pope Francis requested that Kasper present their proposal for a "penitential path" for divorced and remarried Catholics to the Synod of Bishops in 2014.

1999–2010, Vatican Official and Cardinal

In 1998, Pope John Paul II asked Bishop Walter Kasper to make a drastic change: would he come to Rome to be the theological secretary to Cardinal Edward Idris Cassidy in the Vatican's offices for ecumenism and Jewish relations? If so, would he eventually agree to succeed Cassidy, soon due to retire, as the leader to these two offices? Kasper said yes to the pope's requests. In 1999, he packed his belongings, said good-bye to his beloved diocese, and moved to Rome.

As already noted, Walter Kasper invested himself in ecumenism from the start of his work in theology, deliberately pursuing the vision of Johann Adam Möhler whose writings were formative for Kasper. In this activity, Kasper demonstrated his conviction that ecumenism is not peripheral to Catholicism: "Being ecumenical is an essential and inalienable element of being Catholic" (p. 189). In ecumenism, he has cherished not only formal discussions but also close personal relationships. From 1970 to 1989, he interacted daily with the Protestant theologians at the University of Tübingen. Along with his Catholic colleague Hans Küng, he enjoyed regular dinners and discussions with the Reformed theologian Jürgen Moltmann and the Lutheran (Evangelical) theologian Eberhard Jüngel. In his memoir, Kasper mentions his close ties with Jüngel:

> We often met at the podium or in the chancel, most often at Ulm's Münster Church. No one could mistake us for what we were: one of us could not possibly be more Protestant, and the other more Catholic. Still we were close in agreeing on the most decisive matters. When we disagreed, we did this not only with mutual respect but also with the highest regard for the other position. In 1971, on the occasion of an ecumenical meeting at Pentecost in Augsburg, during the time when much was topsy-turvy in the church, we crafted not a confession of faith but a short common account of our faith. (pp. 242-43)

Arriving in Rome in mid-1999, Bishop Kasper immediately contributed to Cardinal Cassidy's efforts at the Pontifical Council for Promoting Christian Unity and also at the Commission on Religious Relations with Jews. Along with undertaking formal activities and conferences, he increased the number of his publications related to Christian unity and to mutual understanding between Jews and Christian. After Cardinal Ratzinger issued the CDF's declaration *Dominus Iesus* (August 6, 2000), Kasper took the initiative to interpret it so that it would not damage the church's efforts in ecumenism and Jewish–Christian relations.

Kasper was initially unsure about how he, as a German, would be received by the representatives of Judaism. Yet, he found himself immediately welcomed by Jewish leaders. "I soon realized that, to my great relief, my German heritage was at no time a problem for my Jewish dialogue partners" (p. 280). In fact, because Kasper quickly formed ties of trust with Jewish leaders, he was asked by them to reinvigorate Jewish–Catholic dialogue after the ambiguous reception among Jews of the commission's document "We Remember: A Reflection on the Shoah" (March 16, 1998). He writes, "Jewish friends came to me and said, 'Let us turn to the future! Let's speak about our common challenges. Let us see how we can build a better future for our children and our children's children. Let us speak about justice and peace in the world, about the struggle against poverty and racism and all forms of discrimination, about respect for human rights and many other similar topics'" (p. 285).

In two years' time, Kasper had won international recognition and respect for his theological leadership in ecumenism and Jewish–Christian relations. Thus, Pope John Paul II named him a cardinal on February 21, 2001. Two weeks later, upon Cardinal Cassidy's retirement, Kasper became the president of the Pontifical Council for Promoting Christian Unity and the chair of the Commission on Religious Relations with Jews. In both of these roles, Kasper sought to affirm the teachings of the Second Vatican Council, Pope Paul VI, and Pope John Paul II. Moreover, he deliberately set out to advance the accomplishments of his predecessors: Cardinals Augustine Bea, S.J. (d. 1968), Johannes Willebrands (d. 2006), and Edward Iris Cassidy. In his high-profile position of leadership, Kasper quickly became known not only for his fine theological mind but also for his energy, warm smile, friendliness, and rich sense of humor.

The death of Pope John Paul II on April 2, 2005, raised a question about Cardinal Kasper's future. At the start of the *sede vacante*, the interval between popes, Kasper submitted— as required by canon law—his resignation from his ecclesiastical roles. Then, as a cardinal elector, he participated in the conclave that on April 19 chose Cardinal Joseph Ratzinger as Pope Benedict XVI. Soon afterward, the new pope asked Kasper to continue in his Vatican leadership, and Kasper said yes. For five more years, he continued to work energetically on behalf of Christian unity and Jewish–Christian dialogue.

During his eleven years in the Vatican's offices, Cardinal Kasper took the approach that he had developed beginning in

1964 as he participated in the Lutheran–Catholic exchange. That is, he deliberately initiated and strengthened personal relationships in ecumenism and Jewish–Christian relations. On the basis of respect and trust, he incorporated four elements into formal discussions: (1) the highlighting of mutually held beliefs, (2) the untangling of misunderstandings, (3) the acknowledging of genuine differences, and (4) the generating of formal statements of new agreements (p. 199). Further, he was clear about the process's aim: new understanding, respect and collaboration among all of the participants. In Kasper's words, "Ecumenism means always beginning anew" (p. 251).

This foundation of personal relationships as the basis of dialogue is evident in all of Kasper's endeavors. It suffices here to highlight his personal ties with some representatives of the Eastern Orthodox churches, the Russian Orthodox Church, the Anglican Church, and Judaism.

The Eastern Orthodox Churches. In his interactions with the Greek Orthodox Church, Kasper formed close ties with Patriarch Bartholomew I and Metropolitan John Zizioulas of Pergamono. In the Coptic Church, he collaborated with Patriarch Schenouda III and Metropolitan Anba Bishoy, with whom he had developed "a relationship of trust." In the Syrian Church, he worked closely with the Patriarch of Antioch Ignatios IV Hazim. Through these interactions, he and his dialogue partners produced joint statements such as the "Document of Ravenna" (2007) and "The Nature, Constitution and Mission of the Church" (2009). As proposed by John Zizioulas, the "Document of Ravenna" differentiates three levels of church governance: "the local level which means the diocese as local church, the regional level which is the patriarch and analogously the national and international conferences of bishops, and the universal level" (p. 223).

The Russian Orthodox Church. With the support of Popes John Paul II and Benedict XVI, Kasper met frequently with Moscow's Patriarch Alexy II and Patriarch Metropolitan Cyril. In May 2008, Kasper accepted Metropolitan Cyril's invitation to visit numerous sacred sites in Russia. During this visit, he came to understand Metropolitan Cyril's observation that the Russian Orthodox Church now finds itself in "a new situation" in relation to other churches. After Kasper took note of the rebuilding of Russia's churches and monasteries, he was told by Patriarch Alexy II, "It is not enough to rebuild the walls of churches; we need a spiritual renewal" (p. 227).

The Anglican Church. In his interactions with representatives of the Anglican Church, Kasper became friends with Archbishop Rowan Williams of Canterbury, whose theological writings Kasper had read with respect over many years. Concerning their initial conversation in 2002, Kasper writes,

> *I was able to meet him at his installation to his episcopal office at the Cathedral of Canterbury. In dogmatic theology he represents a neo-orthodox standpoint. However, he also represents open views on the question of women's ordination and on ethical questions such as homosexuality. I have personally prized him as a significant theologian and as a very spiritual and spiritually rich person. In the English-speaking and international arenas, he is not afraid to express an open and even critical message." (p. 271)*

One of the fruits of Kasper's interactions with Archbishop Williams and other Anglican leaders is the document "Growing Together in Unity and Mission" (2007).

On the basis of his work at the Pontifical Council for Promoting Christian Unity, Kasper wrote numerous publications, among which are *Leadership in the Church* (2003), *That They May All Be One: The Call to Unity Today* (2004), *Sacrament of Unity: The Eucharist and the Church* (2005), *The Church of Jesus Christ* (2008), and *Harvesting the Fruits: Basic Aspects of Christian Faith in Ecumenical Dialogue* (2009). In anticipation of the five hundredth anniversary of the Reformation in 2017, Kasper has accentuated the common goal of "spiritual ecumenism" (p. 190), as envisioned by Abbot Paul Couturier (d. 1953), an international pioneer in Catholic ecumenism. In this regard, Kasper notes, "The question of the goals of ecumenism is one of the most pressing current ecumenical questions" (p. 257). *Catholic–Jewish Relations.* From the outset, as noted above, Kasper formed strong ties with his Jewish dialogue partners. For example, he became a close friend of Rabbi David Rosen, the president of the International Jewish Committee for Interreligious Consultations. In 2005, at the request of Pope Benedict XVI, Kasper went to Jerusalem and invested Rabbi Rosen into the papal knighthood of the Order of Saint Gregory the Great. In his memoir, Kasper notes, "The friendships which have originated in these meetings belong to the most beautiful experiences of the last ten years. The Jewish–Christian dialogue, as every dialogue, ultimately depends on such friendships" (p. 282).

In his discussions with Jewish leaders and also in his public statements on Judaism, Kasper has made it clear that the Christian faith makes no sense without the Jewish faith. Appealing to St. Paul, he emphasizes that the Christian faith is the shoot that originates from its Jewish roots (Rom 11:11–24). In his words, "the church has a special and religious unique relationship to Judaism. . . . One cannot define Christianity without considering its relationship to Judaism. Perhaps one can put it best this way: Judaism and Christianity are not sister churches but sister religions." Implicitly renouncing supersessionism—the view that Christian faith has somehow eliminated the validity of Jewish faith—he adds, "Jews and Christians share the eschatological hope of the prophets. During his historic visit on April 13, 1986 to Rome's Great Synagogue (which was the first visit of a pope there), Pope John Paul II said that Jews are 'our older siblings in the faith of Abraham'" (pp. 279, 281). Inspired and guided by John Paul II's words and personal example, Kasper has tirelessly promoted Jewish–Christian relations. In this effort, he has continually fashioned his thoughts into public lectures and articles such as "Anti-Semitism: A Wound to Be Healed" (2003).

Kasper's friendships with representatives of Judaism have borne fruit in concrete ways. For example, in February 2008, he was able to defuse a potential controversy after Pope Benedict XVI introduced into the Latin Rite for Good Friday a revised petition for the Jewish people. This revised petition's mention of Jesus Christ ignited questions and concerns among Jews. Rabbi Rosen contacted Kasper who immediately published a clarification of the pope's revised petition. On the one hand, Kasper observes that in this prayer, Pope Benedict XVI affirms the Christian understanding of Jesus Christ as the one mediator between God and creation (1 Tm 2:5). On the other hand, Kasper gives the assurance that the pope did not intend to signal a change in the church's respect for God's irrevocable covenant with Jews and Judaism. In particular, he rejects the thought that the Catholic Church would try to evangelize Jews. With this intervention, the cardinal illumined the precise meaning of Benedict XVI's revised petition and simultaneously reaffirmed the church's respect for God's eternal bond with Judaism. In short, Kasper acted in accord with his episcopal motto, "Truth in Love." Two years later, he did so again when he explained that, contrary to Christian fundamentalism, Catholicism has no mission to the Jewish people. (See FCJ.)

Finally, it is noteworthy that, as Cardinal Kasper participated in Jewish–Christian dialogue, he became increasingly aware of the need for Islamic–Christian dialogue and also for trilateral conversations of Christians, Jews, and Muslims (p. 287).

2010—Today, Papal Advisor

On July 1, 2010, Cardinal Kasper retired from the Pontifical Council for Promoting Christian Unity and also from the Commission for Religious Relations with Jews. He had engaged in these challenging roles for eleven years and, at the age of seventy-seven, desired to write the theological books about which he had thought and prayed since becoming a bishop twenty-one years earlier.

One of those books is *Mercy*. Already in the 1970s, Kasper was including discussions of mercy in various writings. Further, he focused on the topic in his 1997 essay "Justice and Mercy" ("Gerechtigkeit und Barmherzigkeit"), developing the idea—drawn in part from Thomas Aquinas—that mercy is not an alternative to but the fulfillment of justice. Interestingly, Kasper wrote this essay as an indirect response to the directive from Cardinal Ratzinger and the CDF that Bishops Kasper, Lehmann, and Saier not implement their pastoral instruction concerning divorced and remarried Catholics. Fifteen years after writing this essay, Kasper in "retirement" incorporated its theme into his book *Mercy.*

During the pontificate of Benedict XVI as well as that of John Paul II, some church officials and laity were persistently portraying the Catholic Church as an immoveable, unchanging rock amid secular society's moral turmoil. Yet, this presentation did not take into account the continuing disclosures of priest sex-abuse scandals and the failure of some bishops to implement the new sex-abuse policies of their respective conferences of bishops. It also disregarded the fact that the church was paying out huge financial settlements to victims of abuse. For example, the US Catholic Church had paid over $3 billion in settlements by 2011. Then, further difficulties in the Vatican came to light.

In 2011, Pope Benedict XVI and the curia began to learn of credible allegations from inside the Vatican concerning sexual improprieties by the curia's clergy, the mismanagement and illegal use of finances by the Vatican's bank, the improper granting of contracts by curial officials, and dysfunctional communications and competitive decision making within the curia. In early 2012, the pope charged three cardinals—Julián Herranz, Jozef Tomko, and Salvatore De Giorgi—to undertake a full inquiry into the Vatican's governance. Benedict XVI received the cardinals' confidential, 350-page report in the autumn of 2012. Soon afterward, the pope directed Vatican officials to issue the formal announcement (February 11, 2013) that he would retire from the papacy effective February 28, 2013.

In early March 2013, the cardinals gathered in Rome for the election of a new pope. Preceding the conclave itself, they held discussions concerning the church's future, the Vatican's complexities, and the personal qualities and skills that they were seeking in Benedict XVI's successor. After the cardinals elected Jorge Mario Bergoglio, they and the world immediately caught a glimpse of this pope's direction: a more pastoral tone within the church, the reform of the curia, and a more dialogical approach to the world. Taking the name of Francis of Assisi, he declared his commitment to the world's poor and to the earth. On March 13, wearing simple vestments as he stood on the papal balcony, he broke with custom as he asked the people in St. Peter's Square to bless him as he assumed the duties of "the Bishop of Rome."

Although Cardinal Walter Kasper likely played a role in the election of Pope Francis, he did not foresee what this election would mean for him. During his first two years of "retirement," he wrote *The Catholic Church: Nature, Reality, Mission* (2011) and *Mercy: The Essence of the Gospel and the Key to the Christian Life* (2012). He may have intended to write other major texts as well. If so, he has had to delay them. At the request of Pope Francis, he has made major contributions to the Synod of Bishops in 2014 and 2015. Amid this responsibility, he also wrote *Pope Francis' Revolution of Tenderness and Love* (2015). In fulfilling the requests of Pope Francis, Kasper has received public criticism from some influential church officials, such as Cardinal Raymond L. Burke, former prefect of the Supreme Court of the Apostolic Signature; Cardinal Carlo Caffarra of Bologna, Italy; and Cardinal Gerhard Ludwig Müller, Prefect of the CDF. In response to criticism, he has explained his positions while also conveying respect for his critics. In short, Kasper has adhered to his episcopal motto: "Truth in Love" (Eph 4:15).

THE COHERENCE OF KASPER'S LIFE
AND THEOLOGY

In his memoir Kasper conveys much about himself when he writes, "I have been able to participate a bit in the *joys and sufferings* of the church in the world. Here and there, our dioceses and the church in Germany were permitted to help bring *hope and light* into the world. I am grateful to have experienced where and how *the heart of faith* beats" (p. 126; our italics). In this statement, the cardinal discloses his commitment to the virtues of faith, hope, and love—three virtues that flow from the Triune God.

This statement by Kasper resonates with a sentence in the first article of the Second Vatican Council's Dogmatic Constitution on Divine Revelation, *Dei Verbum*: this council "wants the whole world to hear the *summons to salvation*, so that through hearing it may *believe*, through belief it may *hope*, and through hope it may come to *love*" (our italics).

The resemblance between Kasper's statement and the sentence on the virtues in *Dei Verbum*, no. 1, is not an accident. The cardinal himself has lived and thought in response to the church's "summons to salvation." In his life and writings, he repeatedly stresses Christian *hope* through the Holy Spirit. As he explains, the source of this hope is *faith* in Jesus Christ, and the fruit of this hope is *selfless love*, *agape*. Further, Kasper associates Christian hope, faith, and love with the God of Jesus Christ.

Hope through the Holy Spirit

Shortly after his eightieth birthday, Cardinal Kasper gave a homily in which he spoke about the centrality of Christian hope in our lives:

> *When I reflected on my eightieth birthday on the good (and less good) that I've done in my life and in my theology, I came to the conclusion that to the degree that I have helped people find hope and joy in God, I achieved at least something. Joy and hope are indeed available to us because God is always new and always greater than our expectations, greater than our hearts. Given*

the divine promise of 'a new heaven and a new earth'
(Rv 21:1), God far exceeds our most keen imaginations.
This hope in God accompanies me also in my old age.
The Old Testament prophet tells us that "the joy of the
LORD is your strength" (Neh 8:10), and the New Tes-
tament announces good and joyful news concerning
"the love of God in Christ Jesus our Lord" (Rom 8:39).
Thus: Be joyful in hope! (BJH, 297–99)

The topic of Christian hope in Kasper's homily was not a new theme for him. Rather, it recurs in many of his writings. Time and again, he refers to the injunction of 1 Peter 3:15: "Always be ready to give an explanation to anyone who asks for a reason for your hope."

At the start of *Jesus the Christ*, Kasper asserts that Christians must continually reflect on the person and work of Jesus Christ so that they can shed light on the wellspring of their hope. He writes, "The remembrance of Jesus and the Christological tradition must be understood as living tradition and thus be maintained in creative faithfulness. Only in this way can living faith develop. Christians should give an account of their hope" (cf. 1 Pet 3:15)" (JDC, 21).

Kasper's emphasis on Christian hope also occurs in his "Autonomy and Theonomy: On the Goal of Christianity in the Modern World" (1980). At the outset, he states, "It is the task of theology to give to all people an account of Christian hope (cf. 1 Pet 3:15). Theology has to explain the non-deducible uniqueness of the hope grounded in God through Jesus Christ in the Spirit through the medium of reason common to all people and thus make the Christian message universally communicable" (ATH, 149).

In the spring of 2013, Kasper spoke about Christian hope in an essay on the aim and method of theology. In his words: "Theology is indebted to the axiom '*Fides quarens intellectum*,' that is, 'faith seeking for understanding' (Anselm of Canterbury). Theology has to be *apologia* of 'the hope' that is within us, and as theologians we have to give 'an accounting' of our faith (1 Pet 3:15)" (HTT, 251).

Kasper's recurring concern for Christian hope did not fall from the sky. It emerged out of the earliest years of his life. He and his sisters received the gift of hope—along with faith and love—from their parents and the church as they grew up in the Nazi state. Recalling what occurred, he writes,

> *So too for me, the twentieth century, into which I was born, did not start as a happy century. No, it was a dark and bloody century. I grew up in Germany during the Nazi time and amid the horrors of the Second World War. But afterward the twentieth century evolved into a century with many ecclesial movements of renewal. Very early, I learned about the liturgical, biblical, patristic, and pastoral renewals that eventually converged in the Second Vatican Council. . . . Vatican II became for me a fixed point of reference. Pope John XXIII understood the council as the dawn of a new epoch, as the beginning of a new spring, and as a new Pentecost. . . . I am convinced that God is present also in our time and in our world. (BJH, 296)*

In this statement, Kasper has deliberately linked hope and "a new Pentecost." Christian hope, as Kasper points out, is not an attitude or personal quality that we adopt on our own; it is not a form of optimism or positive thinking. Rather, hope—along with faith and love—is a gift of the Holy Spirit who, in Kasper's words, is "*the tempest and breath of life. The Spirit is the One who creates, bears, and safeguards everything. The Spirit is, above all, the One who is effective in history and who creates new opportunities and realities*" (KAT, 80). In other words, the Spirit is the divine power who frees or liberates us from all that binds us from within, for example, low self-esteem, and also from without, for example, injustice. It is the Spirit who sustains and directs our hope.

What is Christian hope? It is the gift that disposes and guides us to look for and recognize God's salvific presence and action in our lives, even when things appear grim. Kasper writes,

> Standing in faith in God's faithfulness, human beings orient themselves in hope completely towards the coming reign of God, which has already broken into the world in Jesus Christ. . . . Hope brings freedom from the sense of everyday life's dullness and complacency. Standing vis-à-vis a purely this-world mentality, hope directs itself to the always greater, all-embracing and all-surpassing highest good, to God in God's self as the eschatological fulfillment of human beings and the world. (KAT, 251)

Faith in Jesus Christ

Christian hope arises, Kasper observes, from faith in Jesus Christ. He acknowledges the centrality of Christian faith in his own life and thought by naming his memoir "Where the Heart of Faith Beats" (WHG). He explains that he—as a priest, bishop, and cardinal—has benefitted from the faith of the people whom he wanted to serve. As we have already seen, he holds, "I am grateful to have experienced where and how the heart of faith beats" (p. 126).

Kasper's attentiveness to the vibrant faith of the people with whom he has interacted comes in part from the theological approach that he adopted from the Catholic Tübingen School. That is, according to this method, theologians should learn not only from scholarly inquiry and the church's living tradition but also from the church's current life, that is, from the lives of God's faithful people, including their moral and religious questions, their service of others, and their worship. In this vein, Kasper embraces the Second Vatican Council's retrieval of the church's ancient doctrine of reception, expressed in Lumen Gentium,

no. 25. According to this doctrine, reception is the process by which Christians as individuals, local communities, and councils accept—or do not accept—a teaching, practice, or decision that originated with other ecclesiastical officials and/or governing bodies. This acceptance—or lack therefore—is a process influenced by the Holy Spirit that results in a "sense of the faithful" (*sensus fidei*) that deserves the respect of other believing communities and their governing bodies.

In 1989, Walter Kasper accepted the church's call to become the diocese's bishop because he desired to assume the explicit role of pastor. He writes, "I hoped now more than ever to be able to become what I always wanted to become and to be: a pastor, a spiritual minister" (p. 101). Guided by the doctrine of reception, Bishop Kasper convened advisory boards and diocesan synods and also visited parishes on weekends in order to learn from the laity and priests. "The visits to the parishes, along with the ordinations of deacons and priests, were my most beautiful experiences as bishop. There I could be a pastor, a caregiver for souls. One experiences that there still exists much more *faith* than one might think" (p. 104; our italics).

Although Kasper has made significant contributions to the church in theology, he sees himself primarily as a priest and pastor who engages in theology for the sake of the people and the Christian faith. He writes,

> *Scholarly theology was never my personal goal; theology [for me] was no academic glass-bead game. Even as a professor, I remained what I always wanted to become: priest, pastor, spiritual minister. I wanted to help people in the faith and to help them come to faith. I wanted to offer them arguments so that they could cope with their questions concerning the faith and concerning authentic human and Christian existence. I wanted to show the inner coherence and beauty of the faith. (pp. 82–83)*

What is Christian faith? It is more focused than a general
trust in God. It is a response to and a reliance on the God of
Jesus Christ in the Holy Spirit. Kasper writes, "In *faith*, human
beings anchor their entire existence in God. God is their foundation and content of life. This attitude of trusting faith is only
possible as the answer to the historical revelation of God's faithfulness and reliability" (KAT, 250).

What is the "historical revelation of God's faithfulness and
reliability"? It is God's decisive and complete, salvific self-disclosure in Jesus Christ. Hence, Christian faith relies on the Lord
Jesus. "Christians are those who direct themselves entirely to
Jesus Christ in their thoughts and their lives and who commit
themselves to him. It is primarily through Jesus Christ that we
as Christians know decisively and ultimately who God truly is"
(KAT, 76). Reiterating this understanding, Kasper writes,

> *Christians are those who believe in Jesus Christ, who
> live only in relation to Christ and for Christ, who as
> disciples of Jesus and in friendship with him direct their
> thoughts, intentions, and actions entirely to the God of
> Jesus Christ as they serve other people. Christians are
> those who believe that the fullness of time has appeared
> in Jesus Christ and who view the whole of reality in rela-
> tion to him and for him. Christian belief is therefore not
> a set of teachings and commandments, institutions and
> structures. All of these also have their place. However,
> Christian faith is primarily Jesus Christ and community
> with him. (KAT, 144)*

Kasper's emphasis on friendship with Jesus Christ arises in
part from his own life. As he recalls in his memoir, it was in the
Catholic youth association *Neudeutschland* that he explicitly
learned about friendship with Christ while also experiencing
friendship with Christ in this youth group as well as in his family, parish, and the sacraments, especially the Eucharist. Kasper
writes,

> *Being Christian means in the end and in its depths friendship with Christ. This Christ-centered orientation became important very early to me in the youth association Neudeutschland whose Hirschberg program includes the teaching about the new form of life in Christ.*
> *Certainly, much that one must do day in and day out—and sometimes this is not little—is servant work. One feels caught in a grinder, in an unmerciful calendar of appointments that others schedule for requests and responsibilities which simply come over one and from which one cannot withdraw. This may seem unbearable, especially when one becomes somewhat older and would gladly like a bit more leisure. Yet, this is bearable when one thinks to oneself: "It is a friend who is calling you and for whom you are doing something. He awaits you; you should meet him in the people who want you and need you." (p. 315)*

Love of God and Others

To this point, our discussion of Kasper's life and thought has highlighted two of the three theological virtues. First, Christian hope, nourished by the Spirit, directs Christians to search for God's saving presence and action in their lives and the world. Second, this gift arises from the gift of faith in Jesus Christ. Christian belief brings us into friendship with the Lord Jesus who then sustains us and draws us in the Spirit into union with God. Now we turn to the third gift, agape. As Kasper points out, we know that our hope and faith are authentic when they generate selfless love of God and God's people. As Christians receive God's gifts of faith, hope, and love, they are aware that of the three theological virtues the most important is love. In St. Paul's words, "So faith, hope, and love remain, these three; but the greatest of these is love" (1 Cor 13:13).

To be sure, Walter Kasper is no stranger to agape; he is the recipient of love from his family, friends, associates, and the people of the Diocese of Rottenburg–Stuttgart. In his memoir, he recalls the selfless love that he and his sisters experienced from their parents; he also mentions the importance of his close friends, including the Reverend Josef Schupp, whose sudden death in 1989 left Kasper with a deep sense of loss (pp. 15–20, 85–86). Moreover, Kasper speaks of the agape bestowed on him in his pastoral ministry. During his years as a professor, he deliberately engaged in hospital ministry. While at the University of Münster, he presided at Mass every day of the week at Marienthal Hospital for people with disabilities (pp. 58–59). While at the University of Tübingen, he frequently presided at Mass in Tübingen's hospitals, where nurses brought seriously ill people in their beds into the chapels. Recalling these Masses, Kasper writes, "It was almost a Jesus-like situation similar to those often described in the gospels when Jesus was besieged by people with illnesses" (p. 85). According to Kasper, his pastoral ministry among people, especially with illness or disabilities, has enriched him as a person and also as a theologian. Kasper writes,

During my whole academic life, I was pastorally committed, for example, in the medical clinics in Tübingen and in parishes in Münster, Tübingen and elsewhere. Often, during the week I would wrestle with a theological problem and try to express it in simple words in my Sunday sermon, but I would fail to do so. With this, I would become aware that I myself did not understand the problem well enough. My theological master, Josef Geiselmann—during my last meeting with him in a memorable walk on Tübingen's Österberg—advised me: "When you have understood something, you can express it in simple words." Thus, doing pastoral work and listening to people and their problems has helped me to do my theological work. (HTT, 255–56)

When Kasper moved to Rome in 1999, he became acutely aware of his ties with other people. As he settled into his quarters at the Villa Mater Dei, the residence in Rome for German bishops, and as he took up his work at the Vatican, he received encouragement and assistance from his family, friends, and associates. Yet, he initially felt great loss. He writes,

> *Despite these good circumstances, in the beginning I could have just cried, for I could no longer preside on Sundays at parish Masses. These Masses had meant a great deal to me. Also, priestly-pastoral ministry for non-Italians in Rome is very limited. I hope that I will never need to get completely used to this [lack]. I consider myself blessed that I, as a cardinal, am affiliated not with one of Rome's highly regarded ancient churches but with a parish church, Ognissanti on the Via Appia Nuova, a very lively community where I am always welcome. (pp. 169–70)*

Drawing on his own life, Cardinal Kasper explains that our experiences of selfless love arise from and move us toward the Triune God. Insofar as we allow, we are the recipients of both human agape and divine agape. The God of Jesus Christ is the God who is pure selfless love. Christians encounter this agape, for example, in a sacramental manner at baptism. He writes, "In baptism, humans receive a share in God's life and community. They become so united with God's Son that they, filled by his Spirit, become children of God, of the Father" (KAK, 83).

Moreover, in their daily lives of caring for one another and for others in need, people grow in love of God and of neighbor. In Kasper's words, "Love is that friendship and communion with God in which humans love God 'with whole heart and whole soul' (Mk 12:30) and already now become entirely one with God. . . . Since God loves every human absolutely, true love of God must always go with love of neighbor (see Mk 12:30–31; Jn 13:34; 1 Jn 2:8–10; 1 Cor 13)" (KAT, 251–52).

God's love for us would be questionable, Kasper observes, if God were a nonrelational being, a monad. But such is not the case. God in God's very being is relational, interpersonal. This divine mystery is succinctly expressed in the doxology that we—in union with Christ in the Spirit—address to God, the Father, at the end of the Eucharistic prayer: "Through him, and with him, and in him, O God, almighty Father, in the unity of the Holy Spirit, all glory and honor is yours, for ever and ever. Amen."

Since its inception, the church has proclaimed the God of Jesus Christ as it has baptized its members "in the name of the Father, and of the Son, and of the Holy Spirit" (Mt 28:19). Further, the church formulated its belief in the Triune God in its Nicene Creed, about which Kasper writes,

> *The confession of the Triune God is a profound mystery which no created spirit is able to discover on its own or ever able to comprehend. It is the mystery of a bottomless and overflowing love: God is no solitary being, but a God who gives and communicates the divine self out of the fullness of the divine essence, a God who lives in the communion of the Father, Son and Spirit and who because of that can give and sustain community. Because God is life and love, God can be life and love for us. From all of eternity, God has a place within God for us. In this way, we are—since all eternity—drawn into the mystery of God. In the last analysis, the confession of the Triune God is an interpretation of the statement, "God is love" (1 Jn 4:8, 16b). (KAT, 85)*

In this perspective, the ultimate goal of human life is union with God. Given this primary orientation, Kasper manifests in his words and deeds and person that his foremost intention in his personal relationships, priestly ministry, writings, and ecclesiastical leadership is to give thanks and praise to God. Along with Vatican II, he is committed to passing on God's "summons to salvation" (*Dei Verbum*, no. 1). Not surprisingly, Kasper is concerned neither about himself nor about his ecclesiastical robes and titles. Kasper made this point at the gathering of his family, friends, and associates just prior to the consistory on February 21, 2001, at which Pope John Paul II made him a cardinal. He has recalled,

> *On the evening before this wonderful day, a reception was held in Rome's Campo Santo Teutonico for my relatives, friends and former colleagues at the Rottenburg Cathedral and the University of Tübingen, who had traveled to Rome from Germany. Re-wording a well-known biblical verse, I said in my words of welcome, "What is the point of becoming a cardinal and, in this, losing one's soul?" Above all, I want to remain a human being and a priest. One has to accept that one is addressed in Rome as "Eminence." Yet, in this regard, Rome's taxi drivers know what's best when they address you simply as "Padre." (p. 174)*

Let us conclude. Kasper has written that he is grateful for having experienced where and how "*the heart of faith*" beats around the world and, in this, for bringing "*hope and life*" to people amid their "*joys and sufferings*" (p. 126; our italics). This statement resonates with the Second Vatican Council's explicit intention that the world hear the church's "summons to salvation so that through hearing it may *believe*, through belief it may *hope*, and through hope it may come to *love*" (*Dei Verbum*, no. 1; our italics).

The resonance between Kasper's statement and the council's is deliberate. Having intensely studied Vatican II's documents, Kasper has appropriated them into his life and thought. He has chosen to communicate the council's teachings and vision in his various writings, including in the German bishops' "Catholic Adult Catechism" (KAT). In particular, he has communicated the understanding that, as we live into the mystery of the Triune God, we mature in faith, hope, and love. Conversely, as we mature in faith, hope, and love, we become more fully united with the God of Jesus Christ. Thus, concluding the Catechism's section entitled "God, the Father, the Son and the Holy Spirit," Kasper writes, "The fact of God being from eternity *life and love* in God's Being expresses God's bliss and, for us, it is the reason for our *hope* in the midst of a world of death and hate. In *faith* we are able to know that the ultimate and most profound reality is *life and love* and that we are given a share in this reality through Jesus Christ in the Holy Spirit" (KAT, 85; our italics).

In his mid-eighties, Walter Kasper is a vivacious, youthful man with an immediate personal warmth, a laser-sharp mind, a ready smile and laugh, and a keen sense of humor. Most of all, he manifests in his person the gifts of faith, hope, and love. Living these God-given virtues, Kasper himself is a beacon of hope. His words ring true when he urges, "Be joyful in hope!"

AN OVERVIEW

Let's retrace our steps and then look ahead. First, we asked, who is Walter Kasper? In response, we recounted that Kasper was born 1933 in Heidenheim as Hitler came to power, that he resided in Tübingen from 1952 to 1964 and again from 1970 to 1989, and that since 1989 he has lived in Rottenburg–Stuttgart and in Rome. Over the years, he has shown himself to be an insightful theologian, an exceptional ecclesiastical leader, and, most importantly, a true *Mensch*. On his journey, he pursued his vision: he dedicated his priesthood in 1957 to 2 Corinthians 1:24, "we work together for your joy," and he chose his episcopal motto in 1989 from Ephesians 4:15, "Truth in Love."

Second, we have seen the coherence of Kasper's life and theology as we have noted his recurring emphasis on the three theological virtues. In his writings, Kasper elucidates Christian hope, which he sees sustained by the Holy Spirit. Further, he anchors this hope in belief in Jesus Christ, since faith in the Lord Jesus nurtures hope. Finally, with St. Paul, he stresses that faith and hope bear fruit in agape, in selfless love for God and

God's people and creation. As Kasper explains, this orientation to faith, hope, and love arises from and moves toward the God of Jesus Christ, the God who is the Father and the Son and the Holy Spirit (Mt 28:19).

Given the richness of Cardinal Kasper's life and thought, access into his spiritual–theological writings may seem a daunting task. What is a way to attain a clear, succinct, and focused overview of the riches in Kasper's literary corpus?

Kasper's writings disclose a key, simple truth about their author: he lives in response to and in service of the Gospel. His words manifest the heart and soul of a man who has found the "treasure buried in a field," who has bought it "out of joy" with his life, and who now lives to share this treasure with all people (Mt 14:33). It is this book's aim therefore to give a glimpse of the length, breadth, depth, and spirit of the treasure in Kasper's works.

This book highlights the treasure's *length* by including texts representative of Kasper's writings over forty-five years. Walter Kasper is a prolific writer. As of December 31, 2015, he had written a total of 928 publications, many of which have appeared in numerous languages.

This book lays out the *breadth* of the treasure in Kasper's hands by making available Kasper's texts related to seven fundamental truths of the Christian faith. Each of these basic elements receives its own chapter: (1) "Personal Existence," (2) "Jesus the Christ," (3) "The God of Jesus Christ," (4) "The Holy Spirit," (5) "The Church," (6) "Ecumenism and Jewish–Christian Relations," and (7) "Christian Hope." These seven topics are central to Kasper's thought because he is committed to making intelligible for contemporary believers the "basic truths" of the Christian faith, in particular, the truths that the church confesses in the Nicene Creed.

In three ways, this book probes the *depth* of the treasure in Kasper's writings. First, it includes selections from Kasper's memoir "Where the Heart of Faith Beats." These texts describe the experiences from which arose Kasper's questions, inquiries, and insights into God's revelation as known in the Christian faith through the church. In his work, the cardinal has adhered to Anselm of Canterbury's idea that theology is "faith seeking understanding." For this reason, Kasper's writings are the fruit of the theologian's own faith and the faith of the church in which he has actively participated since birth.

Second, the depth of Kasper's thought comes to light, too, in relation to the documents of the Second Vatican Council. As a theologian, Kasper has sought to elucidate the council's teachings. He writes that "the council's documents presented the direction for my entire, further maturation as a theologian" (p. 53). Kasper's commitment to the teachings of Vatican II is evident in his efforts to illumine and advance the council's thought with regard to the seven topics presented in this book. In order to highlight the affinity between Kasper's thought and Vatican II's teachings, each of this book's chapters begins with a pertinent quotation from a conciliar text.

Third, in his writings, Kasper continually calls attention to the fact that the Christian faith and theology are oriented to mystery. With this recognition, the theologian again evinces his bond with Vatican II as well as the depth of his thought. The conciliar documents repeatedly call attention to mystery, to a reality that we can increasingly understand but never fully comprehend, to a reality whose whole is greater than the sum of its parts. For example, see *Lumen Gentium*, no. 3; *Dei Verbum*, no. 2; *Gaudium et Spes*, no. 10. Similarly, Kasper's writings, as represented in each of this book's chapters, repeatedly acknowledge mystery, for example, the mystery of being human, the mystery of Christ's "person" and "work," the mystery of the Triune God, the mystery of the church, and the mystery of salvation.

Lastly, this book conveys the *spirit* with which Kasper shares the treasure of Christian faith. It does this simply because its texts radiate Kasper's genuine approach to life in light of the Gospel. While acknowledging the limits, tragedies, and evils of human life, Kasper remains oriented to the coming of God's reign and the Parousia of Jesus Christ. With this stance, he does not tire of calling attention to the subtle signs of the Spirit's in-breaking. He urges his readers and listeners to discover the joy and hope that the Gospel imparts. Since he has often emphasized joy and hope, especially in recent years, it is appropriate to conclude this introduction with two of Kasper's statements. He writes:

> *Joy is contagious, whereas laments are repulsive. When we renew the joy of being church that the council intended to inflame, then we shall pass on this joy to others. As this occurs, the church can proceed with a new prophetic power in a rapidly changing and profoundly insecure world. Then, too, the church can be a compass and an encouraging sign of hope for many. (RSO, 293)*

> *Mercy is the new Christian awareness. Mercy gives a foretaste and an anticipation of what we hope for, the coming of the heavenly Jerusalem. Only through mercy does our Christian message of the merciful God become credible, plausible, and authentic. In our church we should start being merciful. In our church we should give good example. One beam of mercy makes the world warmer and brighter for all people. Remain firm in faith! Be joyful in hope! Be merciful with your neighbor! (BJH, 299)*

1

Personal Existence

The joys and hopes, the grief and anguish of the people of our time, especially of those who are poor or afflicted, are the joys and hopes, the grief and anguish of the followers of Christ as well. Nothing that is genuinely human fails to find an echo in their hearts. For theirs is a community of people united in Christ and guided by the Holy Spirit in their pilgrimage towards the Father's kingdom, bearers of a message of salvation for all of humanity. That is why they cherish a feeling of deep solidarity with the human race and its history.

—*Gaudium et Spes*, no. 1

Beginning in his earliest publications, Walter Kasper has highlighted both the potential of our personal existence and also our inability to realize this potential on our own. He holds that humans are able to become free and hence to actualize their potential only as they accept God's gift of salvation, of true freedom that includes mercy. In developing this theological anthropology, he draws on the theology of Thomas Aquinas.

SALVATION AND FREEDOM (1972)

Every attempt by humans to create a better and more just social order occurs under the conditions of injustice and dishonesty, and the attempt itself requires the use of violence. In this attempt, we bear the seed of new conflict and new injustice into the social order. Left to our own means, we cannot break out of this vicious circle of violence and counter-violence, injustice and retaliation. The question of our well-being cannot be resolved from a purely quantitative perspective by always newer and always stronger efforts. Rather, a qualitatively new beginning is necessary. Therefore, humankind in its religions and social utopia has always dreamed of a fundamental change of everything and hoped for a new beginning, not derived from the past. For the sake of society, humans in their hope for salvation want to transcend the dimensions of the existing order. It is at this point that we can speak intelligibly and meaningfully of redemption and grace, and for the sake of humanity we have to. . . .

Salvation is not a supernatural dimension in the sense that it must be added to our human existence. Rather, salvation is the freedom of our freedom; it is freedom's liberation and redemption. Salvation is the condition of the possibility that our freedom will concretely reach its appropriate, meaningful goal. Salvation is the new creation that makes a new history possible for us.

In support of these initially surprising statements, we can easily call upon Thomas Aquinas. For him, the supernatural order is not—as held by modern Scholasticism—an almost independent realm beyond the natural order. For him, supernatural grace is the means by which humans can actually reach their freedom's appropriate goal. These thoughts are not as abstract as they may sound. They express nothing less than that there does not need to exist a fundamental opposition between the modern idea of liberation and the Christian message of redemption. The Gospel's message is a "call to freedom" (Ernst Käsemann). The saving reality of redemption is the concrete reality of freedom. . . .

The concrete space of freedom which humans need in order to be free cannot be established by society alone. According to the New Testament, even those humans who are free from all outer and inner coercion and thus can take charge of their existence are still not yet free. They are lacking in freedom not because they cannot take charge of themselves to a sufficient degree but because they want to take charge at all, that is, because they believe that they can and should manage themselves and their reality itself. This attitude expresses anxiety and concern. Even more, it expresses a fixation on and enslavement to oneself. This lack of freedom is the essence of sin. Theologically speaking, sin is not primarily a moral phenomenon. Sin is an entanglement in oneself, an enslavement to the current state of affairs and apparent security; it is the inability to be free for others and the unforeseen newness of the future. . . . Sin is the inability to love. Therefore, it is the opposite of a human being's salvation and personal wholeness in and with the world.

Freedom is kindled only in an encounter with the freedom of another; freedom is only possible through another's freedom. Someone's salvation therefore depends on the person's encounter with another freed human being. Here is situated the salvific significance of the encounter with Jesus Christ who alone is without sin and entirely free (Jn 8:46; Heb 4:15). With authority, Jesus sets himself above the tradition of the elders (Mk 7:1-13) and teaches as one who has power (Mk 1:22, 27). In an unprecedented freedom, he does not follow the religion's sacred regulations and turns to the God-less people who are socially and religiously shunned. Yet, he is sufficiently free to submit to specific regulations. The last word belongs not to a rigid order but to the sovereign freedom of mercy. . . His message and corresponding conduct made Jesus into the great disrupter of the religious and social order. Nothing is more evident therefore than that the guardians of the religious and social order plotted to eliminate Jesus as soon as possible. The order, the law, required this. Jesus' death on the cross was a last triumph of order; yet it was an even greater victory of freedom. Here freedom becomes truly free. . . . Here the constraint of the enslavement of humans to themselves and to a secure order is broken through. Here a new possibility for a free existence has entered into history.

—EIG, 115–18

Kasper often refers—as the Second Vatican Council does—to the theological notion of mystery. According to this notion, a mystery is a reality that humans can increasingly understand but never fully fathom.

THE MYSTERY OF BEING HUMAN (1973)

The Greatness and Misery of Being Human

Our considerations so far have shown us the greatness and the misery of being human (Blaise Pascal). The greatness of humans comes in transcending everything that exists. Humans infinitely transcend themselves. Their misery nevertheless is that they experience themselves as pitilessly tied into the existing reality: "A human being is only a reed, the most fragile in the world. . . . It is not necessary for the universe to arm itself in order to annihilate them: a breath of wind, a drop of water, is enough to kill them" (Pascal). But precisely in their misery humans become aware once more of their greatness: "The greatness of humans is sublime because they recognize themselves as miserable. A tree knows nothing of its misery. Therefore, only that which knows itself to be miserable is miserable; but that is greatness, to know that one is miserable" (Pascal). That is a remarkable statement and a quite stimulating sentence; for in the face of all claims to untroubled happiness free of suffering—claims and expectations that modern advertising tirelessly urge us to hold—Pascal states that true human greatness consists in suffering. . . .

The existential situation of humans is the mean between two extremes. Humans are the creatures of the boundary (Thomas Aquinas) between nature and spirit, time and eternity, God and the world. . . . Because of this existential situation between the extremes a human being's essential nature is profoundly ambiguous. The expression "it's only human" can be used to describe our lowest and meanest behavior: all possible weaknesses and vices count as human. But we also use the term human to mean what is the most noble in our world: generosity, sacrifice, understanding, compassion, forgiveness. Humans are a riddle and a mystery: "There are many marvels and nothing more marvelous than a human being" (Sophocles). Human freedom has its foundations in this openness and lack of pre-determination. But humans cannot actually stay in this openness and ambiguity. If they look into the abyss of their own potentialities, they are overcome by "the dizziness of freedom" (Kierkegaard). Fear seizes them, and they try to cling to what is finite, visible, tangible, and calculable. By doing so, they choose what is not and are given over to non-being (cf. Rom 8:20). Humans as a whole and as individuals—such as we actually experience them and ourselves—have already alienated themselves from their greatness and destiny. As tragedy shows, this alienation holds sway over us as an unavoidable fate. All attempts to escape from this situation by one's own power fail. Since we are all subject to the conditions of injustice, violence, hatred, and falsehood, we must make use of violent means to bring about a just order. Hence, into every new order we carry the seed of new injustice, the seed of embitterment and violence. So we exist in a genuine vicious circle of guilt and expiation, injustice and revenge. A qualitative leap, a fundamentally new beginning is necessary, one that cannot be derived from the conditions of what has gone before.

Here we come face to face with the profoundest mystery and the actual paradox of being human. The experience of greatness is tied to the experience of misery. Hence, we humans can never attain our greatness by our own resources. The essential lines of our existence cannot be extrapolated to infinity; they cross each other and turn our existence into a contradiction. What then is a human being? A torso, a fragment? Does the last word rest with ancient and modern tragedy, with ancient and modern skepticism?   —GEH, 42–56

In Kasper's judgment, the foundational dynamism of our age is the freedom or liberation of individual persons and also of communities and societies. This emphasis on freedom is our contemporary world's strength and also its weakness.

BEYOND BELIEF IN PROGRESS (1978)

The contemporary crisis is the crisis of the foundational principle of modernity. At the beginning of the modern age, people discovered their freedom in an entirely new way. They discovered that they were not handed over by fate to the forces of nature and to the long-standing political institutions, but that they were the autonomous lords of their own destinies. Modern natural science and technology gave them the means to design their own future. As a consequence, humans have lived through far more changes in the past two hundred years than in the previous two millennia. Belief in progress shaped the eighteenth and nineteenth centuries.

This belief in progress was already shaken at the start of the twentieth century by the First World War. Oswald Spengler wrote his widely-read book *The Decline of the West* [1918]. At the same time, the emerging philosophy of existentialism attempted to reflect on the contemporary world's unleashed insecurity and anxiety. The Second World War's horrors showed still more profoundly the ambiguity and the misuse of technological progress. . . . Science and technology, which should serve human freedom, now threaten to proceed beyond human comprehension and to become a second tier of fate. Belief in progress is more or less changing into a future shock. . . .

Out of this, there arises a spiritual disorientation and a lack of purpose, which in the long run will be fatal. For humans do not only have hope but are beings of hope. No human being can live, love, work, and act without hoping and relating to the future. It is part of human existence to be both gifted with oneself and given as a task to oneself. For humans, the future must be constituted of openness; it must be an arena of freedom. The future is therefore not primarily what will occur tomorrow and the next day; rather, it is a constitutive dimension of today. The future determines today's "where to" and "what for" and hence our raison d'être in the present. The future exists in the present moment, and it is the purpose of the present moment. Whenever hope in the future is lost, life becomes pointless. The question for the future is therefore the locus and paradigm of the question of the salvation of human beings. Hope is the epitome of salvation.

No one is more challenged by today's state of affairs than Christians. They are now being asked to give an intelligible account of the hope that abides in them [1 Pt 3:15]. They must validate the potential of hope that is part of the Christian faith in the face of the contemporary world's issues and anxieties, its conflicts and aspirations. —ZUG, 9–10, 12–13

According to Kasper, contemporary thought—beginning with the Enlightenment's emphasis on rationality—is confounded by evil, by that which is senseless or irrational in itself. Faced with a situation or event that is evil, the modern mind oscillates between avoidance and fascination. However, Christian faith recognizes evil and provides a language by which to face it. In the 1970s, many people took note of the issue of evil in the film The Exorcist *(1973) and its sequels.*

THE ISSUE OF EVIL (1978)

The Dilemma

Issues related to demonic possession and exorcism always challenge our intellects. The sensational accounts that appear from time to time in the media would not be possible if the reported phenomena did not arouse a secret fascination in us. Elements of an archaic, magical and mythical world—that we've partially overcome, partially suppressed and submerged in our unconscious—suddenly come to consciousness and trigger sub-conscious anxieties, a thrill of curiosity, and to some extent a seemingly self-secure criticism. Yet, that which is strange to our contemporary, rational view of reality also prompts careful consideration.

The problem of evil and its resolution face us today as they did in earlier times. In a strange dialectical process, the increasing rationality in our stance toward reality breaks into new forms of irrationality. Above all, this increasing rationality results not only in good; it also enables evil to organize itself and puts into its hands new, unanticipated, atrocious possibilities. In this regard, names such as Auschwitz, Hiroshima, Gulag Archipelago, and others speak for themselves. The issues conveyed in ancient myths about evil are still our questions. But how do we go about answering them?

Traditional theology more or less adopted the corresponding themes in sacred scripture and the church's tradition which speak of the devil, Satan, demons, and evil "powers and principalities" [Rom 8:29]. But beginning with the Enlightenment, this kind of discourse has been fundamentally called into question.... Today the question arises, how should these themes be interpreted? Are they referring to real, personal beings, or are they culturally conditioned personifications of real powers of evil? ...

A simple rejection of traditional teachings, a "farewell to the devil," is hardly possible. The phenomenon of evil is an unavoidable given in our experience. No pseudo-Enlightenment optimism can dismiss the fact that there are abysses in reality which challenge Christian belief and Christian theology.... The experience of evil can be just as much an argument for hope in redemption by God as an argument against God. It can even be a reason to blaspheme. For what kind of God is it who creates a world in which evil occurs among humans not only in the form of specific, almost loveable personal flaws but also often adopts the form of perverse malice that can assume structural and institutional expression? What kind of God creates a world in which there exists an unflinching demonic will to power, to indulgence and to possessions, to demonic cruelty and to vandalism? Talk about God which does brave such questions remains abstract, thus lacking authenticity and actual significance....

Philosophical Considerations

The entry point for most people today to the problem of evil is the path of experience. People say that evil is a reality in human experience. There exist the abysmal, the absurdities, the monstrosities, the destructive, and the faceless. All of this is mentioned not only in the Bible and church tradition but also in modern literature (e.g., foremost by G. Bernanos and F. Mauriac but also by F. Kafka, A. Camus, B. Brecht, and others) and in the human sciences (e.g., depth psychology, sociology, ethology, and especially para-psychology). In contemporary philosophy, one thinks of E. Bloch, L. Kolakowski and P. Ricoeur. . . . The question is whether a notion of the devil is a binding, even a truly suitable category of meaning for this experience. . . .

Our fundamental thesis is this: the realm in which the problem of evil can be addressed in a philosophically meaningful way is the realm of human freedom. Distinct from physical evil, *malum physicum*, there is moral evil, *malum morale*, which occurs only where there exists freedom and thus accountability and responsibility. . . .

Moreover, physical evil and moral evil point back to metaphysical evil, *malum metaphysicum*, which is related to the world's finitude. With this reference of the problem of evil to metaphysical evil, that is, to the limits given by the world's finitude, we reach the last and encompassing horizon, the metaphysical question about existence itself, about being. The question of evil places us before the question about the meaning of being in general. There emerges this question: is finite existence good in itself? Is there validity to the classical axiom that *ens et bonum convertuntur*, that being and good are identical? Or, is finite existence divided in itself, possessing an inclination to evil? . . .

To approach the problem of evil in this encompassing manner is implicitly to speak about the theological dimension of the question about evil. For the question about the meaning of existence is identical, theologically speaking, to the question about the meaning of creation. Therefore, from a theological perspective, we must again transcend the dimension of human freedom into a more encompassing horizon, namely, into the dimension of God's freedom.

Theological Considerations

The theological response to the question of evil, which at this point is more in depth and encompassing, does not result from a process of philosophical speculation. For a theologian, the response is specified in the Gospel. The Gospel's central message is this: God has shown once and for all that in Jesus Christ God is the Lord of all reality, the Lord over life and death, the Lord also over all "powers and principalities" of evil. In faith, we have the certainty that at the end God will be "all in all." . . . Therefore, the basic Christian stance vis-à-vis evil is not angst but hope in evil's final overcoming.

Next, the theological development of the doctrine of evil unfolds within the doctrine of creation, which is anchored in the central confession of God's eschatological and universal saving action in Jesus Christ. At the end, God can be "all in all" only because God is from the very beginning the reality that determines everything else. There exists no contrary dynamism along with God. There exists no chaos along with God, independent of God. Belief concerning creation holds therefore that everything which exists only exists because God—acting freely out of love—gives it a share in God's own being.

Thus, there results a second fundamental statement concerning the reality of evil: Strictly speaking, evil does not have its own existence. Freely willed by God, called into existence by God, and being sustained by God, all reality is fundamentally good. Although evil may posture as intimidating and brutal, it represents theological vanity. Making itself great and puffing itself up, evil is nevertheless empty, hollow and void. . . .

The possibility of evil results therefore not from creation's incompleteness and frailty but, on the contrary, from its grandeur and dignity, from that which is the most perfect in creation:

the reality of ultimate freedom, the reality of personal existence. This means that our initial question concerning "evil" or the "evil one," more precisely, "evils," cannot remain theologically generic. Purely objective talk about evil that lacks a finite personal subject is theologically untenable because—as its ultimate upshot—either it presents God as the originator of evil and thus demonizes God, or it has to posit an evil, primal principle along with God and thus disposes of God as God, as Almighty. If we dismiss both of these options, then there remains only the option of conceiving of evil as an outcropping of creaturely freedom.

Thus, a third fundamental statement concerning evil arises from the historical determination of reality in general and of the reality of evil in particular. By doing what's evil, creatures arrogate the right to set loose those options which God has excluded from the reality of creation. In this way, they dissolve the cosmic order of the cosmos and unleash chaos. In evil, created beings give power to a possibility that God excluded as void. Evil is the power of non-being, of the chaotic and destructive in the world.

—TPB, 41–54

The contemporary world is experiencing a crisis: on the one hand, it embraces the value of freedom or liberation for individuals, communities, and society; and yet, on the other hand, it is frustrated in its efforts to realize freedom in people's lives; society; and economic, political and social systems. The way forward involves personal transformation and the leap into Christian faith.

CRISIS AS OPPORTUNITY (1980)

According to the Second Vatican Council, our epoch is characterized by a transition which is unfolding with many conflicts and tensions, moving from a static view of the order of reality to an evolutionary, dynamic and historical view. History means that reality is not a pre-determined, sacred cosmos but a creative task entrusted to humans. At the beginning of modernity, humans made themselves into the masters of reality with the intent to transform it in a truly gigantic undertaking with respect to their needs and plans. In this endeavor, they made progress in many humanitarian arenas. Today, however, at the end of these developments, we stand as the sorcerer's apprentice who cannot get rid of the spirits that he has previously conjured. Our scientific–technological civilization threatens to overwhelm us, to spin out of control, becoming a fate of a second order.

Today we are experiencing anew the finitude, the powerlessness and the contingency of being human. We experience it, above all, when we embark on the endeavor of building a more equitable social order. Whenever we go up against injustice and power, we are operating under the conditions of injustice. We often have to employ power ourselves and hence carry the seed of new injustice, of new bitterness into the desired, new order. We find ourselves in a vicious circle. If our hope is not to be in vain, then we must start from a new beginning that is not deducible from history but is marked by justice and reconciliation. We cannot save ourselves; salvation is a gift.

Within historical thought and considering our current, acute crisis, the biblical message of salvation in Jesus Christ and the new beginning in him attains an entirely new relevance. A Christology "from above" is precisely the answer to the question which was asked from below, *de profundis* [Ps 130]. Most interestingly, our approach to asking historical questions brings us closer to the historical, biblical way of thinking than was possible based on a Hellenistic approach. The contemporary crisis can be a Kairos, a moment of opportunity, for developing Christology in a historical and personal perspective. We are still standing at the beginning which is, I think, a hopeful beginning.
—NGC, 32–33

In 1980, Cardinal Kasper addressed the gathering of German Catholic youth in Berlin concerning all people's yearning for love. He explained that humans as individuals, communities, and societies desire to receive love and to give love to others. Yet, this desire is ultimately fulfilled only by God. In giving this address, Kasper spoke in West Berlin, which was then sur-rounded by the Berlin Wall, a symbol of distrust and alienation. He did not know, of course, that on November 9, 1989, the people of East Berlin would overrun the Berlin Wall.

AGAPE AT THE HEART OF REALITY (1980)

A symbiosis of religion and society existed in all pre-modern cultures and into the nineteenth century. Fundamental human and societal regulations are legitimated by all religious beliefs. Antiquity's philosophical teaching on natural law sought to provide a rational explanation for these universal, religious conceptions. In this way, it subordinated the positive order to the critical norm of an inaccessible law that was binding even upon the rulers and that could be validly used against them, if need be. The church Fathers accomplished a synthesis between the thought concerning natural law and the Christian message of the reign of God, which at the same time is the reign of justice, truth, peace, and love. Out of this synthesis emerged European humanism in Europe's culture, the humanism which—undergoing many transformations—reached into modern classicism well into the nineteenth century.

In modernity, though, European humanism emancipated itself from its ecclesial, Christian and religious framework. This process of increasing secularization—which happened in several developmental spurts—was partially due to the schism of the sixteenth century. After Christian belief could no longer serve as the unifying bond in society, one was compelled to place community life and peace on a religiously neutral basis. In this new situation, religious belief turned into a private matter, and the structure of the state and society became non-religious and non-theistic. The world became God-less, while religious belief, Christianity and the church became increasingly world-less and devoid of everyday reality.

As this occurred, law, freedom and conscience—which are fundamental Christian ideas—were isolated from their original religious and Christian framework, and they were critically employed against Christianity. As a result, they became "dis-located." Christian notions are extremely vulnerable to crises, because wherever these ideas and others such as culture, nation and race are turned into absolutes, they necessarily become totalitarian and result in the suppression of human freedom. Thus there emerged what the philosophers Hockheimer and Adorno have called the "dialectic of the Enlightenment" in which rationality again and again turns into blind irrationality. The most debased instance of this departure from Christian culture and change into barbarism was Germany's National Socialism. Also, Marxism, although in a different way, displays secularized and perverted elements of Christian hope for salvation. In the end, our entire scientific and technical civilization has roots in the Bible's understanding of creation. However, when the cultural task of humankind is isolated from its religious basis and boundaries, there results this kind of cynical exploitation of nature, which ultimately leads both to the exploitation of humans by other humans and to the destruction of the humane conditions for life. . . .

In light of the threats to and the dissolution of Christian-shaped humanism in the modern history of liberation, it becomes evident that for a long time the church did not recognize the liberation movement's Christian roots and its legitimate aspirations. As a result, the church's reaction to the liberation movement was at first defensive, engaging in *apologia* and seeking a restoration.

In its working paper, "The Church and Human Rights" (1974), the Pontifical Commission for Justice and Peace admitted that the church's reaction to the modern human-rights movement was characterized too often by reluctance, objections and reservations. Indeed, it speaks of the open enmity and condemnation by popes. Unfortunately, this is all too true. As a result of the church's defensive stance to modernity, the nineteenth century saw the rise of "Integralism," a sort religious totalitarianism aimed at deriving the answers to all questions concerning private and public life directly from the Christian faith and also at subjecting all realms of culture to norms determined by the church's teaching office. This reaction resulted in a rigidly hierarchical Catholicism that was, at the same time, closed in on itself and also closed off from developments in society. It yielded a Catholicism with an excessive inclination to preserving the status quo rather than to adjusting.

Yet, already in the nineteenth century, a reversal became evident among various lay movements and lay organizations, a change supported by Pope Leo XIII in church teaching. The Second Vatican Council helped these tendencies reach a breakthrough. Drawing on the teachings of Thomas Aquinas, the council explicitly acknowledged the autonomy of secular realms. It differentiated, though, autonomy rooted in creation itself from atheistic autonomism (see *Gaudium et Spes*, nos. 36, 41, 56). With this differentiation, it rejected secularism and also Integralism and clericalism which does not recognize the laity's primary competence in the secular arenas (*Lumen Gentium*, nos. 21, 36; *Gaudium et Spes*, no. 43). In its Declaration on Religious Freedom, *Dignitatis Humanae*, the council also accepted and gave Christian legitimation to the essential aspirations of the modern understanding of the person as a subject. In this, it moved from postulating the objective right of the truth to acknowledging the subjective right of the person. Yet, the council did not suspend the binding character of objective truth to which personal conscience has to orient itself. Rather, it recognized that the truth establishes its claim by virtue of being the truth and through the mediation of conscience (*Dignitatis Humanae*, nos. 1, 3). . . .

Everything now calls for a new understanding of the relationship—or, more precisely, for a renewal of the classical understanding of the relationship—between Christian belief and modern society, between Christian salvation and human well-being. . . .

The fundamental insight of humanism in antiquity and also in the Bible is that humans are finite beings. Humans are truly human only when they do not try to be like God, when they acknowledge the limits set for humans and do not fall into hubris. In their finitude, human beings cannot "attain" the realization of their personal fulfillment on their own. Rather, they depend on being fulfilled and loved by an "other." In love, humans experience the grandeur and the misery of their human existence: grandeur, because love bursts the constraints of the human "I," leading a human being beyond human existence, and in this way granting fulfillment, happiness and blessedness; misery, because love is indeed dangerous and fragile. It can go wrong in thousands of ways; it can be abused and perverted. Even in success, love entails the melancholy of fulfillment; it brings with it the deep longing for a still greater and still deeper fulfillment. In the successes and failures of love, humans experience themselves as mysteries, as questions which they themselves cannot answer. For ultimately, they await and hope for an unconditional yes of love, an unconditional acceptance that only God can give. As Augustine observed, it is only in God that the restlessness of the human heart will find its definitive rest.

In the perspective of Christian faith, Jesus Christ is the definitive answer to the question which humans are in themselves. For Jesus Christ—the definitive self-revelation of God, the image of God (2 Cor 4:4; Col 1:15)—is at the same time the fulfillment of the human image of God (Gn 1:26), the new Adam (Rom 5:14; 1 Cor 15:45) in whom God has decisively revealed humans to themselves (*Gaudium et Spes*, no. 22; *Redemptor Hominis*, no. 10).   —WKC, 26–32

This text is continued in Chapter 2, where it is entitled "The Sacrament of Divine Agape (1980)."

Kasper agrees with the view that while contemporary society is religionless, many people today possess, in fact, the potential to respond to God's salvific presence and action in their lives. In articulating this thought, he knows that it was expressed by

Alfred Delp, S.J. (d. 1944) and Dietrich Bonhoeffer (d. 1945) as each of them awaited execution in Nazi Germany.

TODAY'S SEARCH FOR GOD (2008)

The image of the pilgrim is multi-layered. One can currently see a renaissance of pilgrimages in Europe. I have the impression, too, that many people are on an inner pilgrimage, that is, on the search for self and God, and in this they are not always experiencing the help of the church. The parishes must ask themselves whether they present themselves as closed institutions rather than as places where seekers are welcome. The same pertains to people who in their lives have made many detours or are perhaps after a time of disorientation cautiously seeking again a place in the church. These people are in a sense pilgrims or converts. . . .

I consider it a loss that due to the appropriate emphasis on the Eucharist as the high point of ecclesial life other forms of worship and the celebration of sacramental activities have more or less disappeared from the everyday life of the church. In any case, a center point is only a center point when there exists a surrounding realm with different points of proximity to and distance from that center.

As humans, we depend on signs, especially in our often very secular daily lives. Many such signs have a community-forming power. I remember still my own childhood and youth in which there existed a rich world of symbols and signs which gave it structured time and a rhythm. Many of our contemporaries are seeking such signs and finding them often outside the church in New-Age movements or in the religious forms of the Orient. The Eucharist is for them a high form to which they initially have perhaps no entry.

One can think of many examples: celebrations of God's Word, blessings, the laying on of hands, baptismal remembrances, the Stations of the Cross, processions, guided meditations, and also the rosary prayed in common. At this time, many things are being tried out. There have to be many points of entry.

—WHG, 158–59, 161

While in prison awaiting his execution by the Nazis, the Jesuit Alfred Delp expressed thoughts similar to [those of Dietrich Bonhoeffer]. Reflection on their writings shows that neither Dietrich Bonhoeffer nor Alfred Delp held that it is pointless today to bear witness to Jesus Christ. Just the opposite! Bonhoeffer tried to say that we should not preach God as the "God-of-the-gaps" who intervenes as the almighty *Deus ex machina* when we are at a loss. For Bonhoeffer, the modern development had done away with this false view of God and thus made space for the God of the Bible who in worldly powerlessness attains power and depth.

Bonhoeffer points to the cross on which God in weakness and powerlessness has manifested God's helping and healing power for us. Like Delp, he is convinced that the "God for us" and humble, representative Christian discipleship and a church which exists "for the other" are the only chance for Christianity in today's world. "The life of Jesus Christ has not yet come to an end on this earth. Christ lives on in the life of his disciples."

It is rewarding to ponder what this insight means for a new social form of a church that casts itself as a humble servant-church, which bears witness not through worldly splendor and power but through its service. —WHG, 165

Every person is intended by God. Kasper stressed this understanding in his homily at the Mass on the occasion of his seventy-fifth birthday.

Our roots go far back, truly back into eternity. Every one of us is an eternal thought of God, thought with great love. No one is just an accident, a whim of fate, a small cog or small part in the machinery of the world. . . .

Each of us is personally thought of and chosen; each one has a personal calling, a task, a place, and a specific destination. In this regard, there is a red thread in each life, a red thread that we ourselves have not woven, that we shall fully and decisively first know when we have arrived in eternity. At that moment, we will stand as though in front of an embroidery. Looking at it from below, everything is a tangle of threads. Turned over, however, after our stiches are done, only then does the pattern become evident. This pattern includes even our personal flaws. . . .

We are destined not to become a cardinal or God knows what, but "to be holy and blameless before God in love" [Eph 1:4].

—WHG, 313

SACRED SIGNS (2012)

A secular age. The world has become secular. Religion [in this age] may have relevance for the individual, in private, but there is no room for the sacred in the public sphere. Sacred signs, sacred places, and sacred times have lost their unifying and hence binding meaning. Today, one attempts to ban sacred signs from the public sphere—and often, paradoxically, in the name of tolerance.

This is an exciting, new situation because the sacred and the distinction between the sacred and profane are a foundational element of human history. In this regard, I would like to mention two renowned theologians: Émile Durkheim and Mircea Eliade. The latter wrote: "All the definitions of religion have a common element: all of them set—in one way or another—the sacred and the religious life against the profane and the secular life." The sacred is the space set apart, separated from the profane, the profane is the space in front of the *fanum*, the sanctuary. The biblical language uses the same distinction. The biblical word holy (Hebrew *kados*, Greek *temenos*, Latin *sanctus*) derives from separating, demarcating and differentiating.

If the sacred and the profane relate to each other in this way, then it is evident that the loss of the sacred entails the loss of the profane. Without the profane space in front of a *fanum*, the sacred, there is no sacred space separated from the *profanum*. It is impossible to forget, deny, abolish, or fight the sacred and at the same time to keep the profane. Both will disappear. We cannot shake off an archetypal phenomenon like the sacred [expecting] that everything else will remain unaffected. There will remain an awareness of that which is missing.

Today, many do not know anymore an awe of the sacred, the ineffable, nor the fascination of glorious splendor. To use a famous word of Max Weber: our world is de-mystified. It became factual and pedestrian, often also mundane and super-ficial. There where the distinction between sacred and profane is erased, the world is indifferent, monotonous, drab and grey. Where once there was transcendence into a mystically other, wonderful and divine world, there is today quite often boredom and weariness, and there where were the gods, repeatedly reigns the fear of ghosts.

What is left, after the loss of the sacred, is a certain melan-choly and nostalgia, the sense of something missing. The con-temporary interest in esoteric literature is huge, as one can see in any book store. Many young people live in a Harry-Potter fantasy world, a place filled with sorcerers, witches and non-hu-man beings. On a higher level, art is replacing religion. Not the churches but the museums are the new temples. This is also a phenomenon among young people, a fact which should give cause for concern.

Increasingly, we are becoming aware of that which is missing in our lives. More people than we might think are on the quest, searching for holy ground. They are seekers and pilgrims, quite often attracted to and also deterred by the sacred. Many of them have not yet crossed the threshold of the church; for many, it is too high; many also feel not invited or even rejected. They are so to speak in the courtyard of the pagans. The Temple of Jerusa-lem had such an area, the Courtyard of the Gentiles. It was sur-rounded by a magnificent portico; at the same time, a stone wall separated it from the inner temple district. Under the penalty of death, only Jews were allowed to enter there. The good news of

the New Covenant was that the cross of Christ has broken down
this wall. Now, all have access to the sanctuary, all are fellow
citizens of the saints and members of the household of God (Eph
2:14–19). Even the curtain of the Holy of Holies is torn by the
death of Christ (Mk 15:38).

This event has been interpreted as abolishing the distinction
between the sacred and the profane. But especially Paul's letter
to the Ephesians, which describes the razing of the wall, also
talks clearly about the foundational sign of baptism through
water, which cleanses and sanctifies and thereby gives access to
the Holy God (Eph 5:26). Even according to the Letter to the
Ephesians, it is not possible simply to stroll from the secular
world into the realm of the holy. There is a required cleansing
and sanctification. Hence, in the New Testament, the distinction
between the secular and the holy is not abolished but rather
re-defined. . . . It is important that we search for this new biblical
understanding of the holy and the profane, of sacred times and
sacred places. We have to do this for the sake of those who are
still in the Courtyard of the Gentiles. And, I think that all of us
are there, in some sense.   —HEI, 10–13

2

Jesus the Christ

In reality it is only in the mystery of the Word made flesh that the mystery of humanity truly becomes clear. For Adam, the first man, was a type of him who was to come, Christ the Lord. Christ the new Adam, in the very revelation of the mystery of the Father and of his love, fully reveals humanity to itself and brings to light its very high calling. . . . In him God reconciled us to himself and to one another, freeing us from the bondage of the devil and of sin, so that each one of us could say with the apostle: the Son of God "loved me and gave himself for me" (Gal 2:20). By suffering for us he not only gave us an example so that we might follow in his footsteps, but he also opened up a way. If we follow this path, life and death are made holy and acquire a new meaning

—*Gaudium et Spes*, no. 22

Kasper's meditative essay "The Mystery of Being Human" (see Chapter 1) concludes with a reflection on the mystery of Jesus Christ. It develops the statement of Gaudium et Spes, *no. 22 that Jesus Christ "fully reveals humanity to itself and brings to light its very high calling."*

ECCE HOMO! (1973)

Behold the Human Being! [Jn 19:5]

When human greatness and misery are taken seriously, when neither hope nor despair are set up as an absolute, when therefore one tries to do justice to a human being as a whole, then the question of God must be asked. It is extremely superficial to think that our modern world makes religion more and more superfluous. It is precisely our modern civilization that in all likelihood will, with the suffering it itself has produced, arouse religious hope to a yet unimaginable extent. The soul of religion is indeed nothing other than "the longing for the completely other" (Max Horkheimer), a longing displayed in the ultimate depth of the dialectic between greatness and misery. "It is from dissatisfaction with earthly fate that recognition of a transcendent being draws its strongest power. . . . In religion the wishes, longings and accusations of innumerable generations are deposited" (Horkheimer). "The only way philosophy can still be defended in the face of despair is as the attempt to regard all things as they present themselves from the perspective of redemption" (Theodore Adorno). Only God, who controls the conditions of all reality, is able to transform this reality without doing violence to it. Only God, who is Lord over life and death, can, in the doom of death, be the source for hope against all hope (cf. Rom 4:18). Hence, at its profoundest the mystery of being human touches the mystery of God. A human being is "the poor reference to the mystery of abundance" (Karl Rahner).

The Christian confession of Jesus Christ means nothing else than that in Christ the mystery of a human being, of human greatness and misery, has become the grammar and the expression of the mystery of God in a unique and yet universally valid manner. It is not as if we could derive fulfillment from our longing and hope: the mystery of being human would then be ignored while the depths of the mystery of God would be misunderstood. The mystery of our human existence poses a question.

All we can do is either to accept in faith or to reject in unbelief the factual answer of the message of Jesus Christ. Every form of argument must take on the character of appeal, encouragement and persuasion.

What is convincing about the form and message of Jesus Christ is nevertheless that it stands the test with regard to both the greatness and the misery of human beings. Indeed, it is only through Jesus Christ that human greatness and misery are revealed to us in their profundity as in their inner meaning-fulness. "It is equally important for humans to know this and that; and it is equally dangerous for humans to know God with-out knowing their misery as it is for them to know their misery without knowing the redeemer who is able to save them from it. Knowing only one of these will lead either to the conceit of the philosophers, who have known God and not their misery, or to the despair of the atheists, who know their misery without the redeemer." (Pascal) Through Jesus Christ, humans can come to know both God and their misery. Jesus of Nazareth as one who was tortured, mocked, cursed, and put to death, though innocent, is the symbol of all "the humiliated and insulted" (Dostoyevsky).

Divine revelation has shown that God is the "God of humans" (cf. Heb 11:16). . . . Thus, one must apply to the cross, as Shell-ing did, Anselm of Canterbury's definition of God: "[the cross is] that greater than which cannot be conceived." This is the only possible definition of God and also of humans.

The "message of the cross" (1 Cor 1:18)—"a stumbling block to Jews and foolishness to Gentiles" (1 Cor 1:23)—is distinctly Christian. As long as Christianity wants to go on being Christi-anity, it is only from the cross that it can find its destiny and its meaning for the world. But doesn't it make us wonder to observe how much this cross is constantly derided not only in the history of humanity but also in the history of Christianity itself up to today? It is derided not so much by theoretical discussions but rather by practical action that knows only one thing: making one's power prevail. "Anyone who sees this, and considers it is not amazed that things aren't going well for Christianity" (J. Möller). Yet, it is in the cross that all Christianity's chances and opportunities are to be found today as it has always been. This sign of contradiction—that resists all harmonization—is not the crucifixion and humiliation of humanity. In this sign, the mystery of being human—in a completely un-deduced and unique manner—has found its universally valid and ultimately definitive expression. In it, all who accept it as their own cross, are given a new way to be human in an inhumane world.

—GEH, 51–56

During the early 1970s, Kasper worked with his lectures in Christology at the University of Münster and at the University of Tübingen as he wrote his Jesus the Christ. *This widely respected book was published in the same year, 1974, as two other noteworthy Christological texts in Catholic theology: Hans Küng's* On Being a Christian *and Edward Schillebeeckx's* Jesus. *In his comprehensive work, Kasper integrated critical exegesis of the Bible, historical study into the church's living tradition, and a consideration of contemporary issues and ideas into his systematic inquiry into the "person" or identity of Jesus Christ and also into the "work" of Jesus Christ, that is, into Jesus Christ as savior or redeemer.*

THE PERSON OF JESUS CHRIST (1974)

The church's fundamental confession, as the Council of Chalcedon formulated it, is that Jesus Christ is true God and true human being in one person. . . . Jesus Christ in person is the mediator between God and humans (1 Tm 2:5) and the new covenant (1 Cor 11:25; Lk 22:20). . . .

The unity of God and humankind in Jesus Christ is one of the fundamental Christological expressions in scripture. It is characteristic for the earthly Jesus that he speaks and acts as one who stands in God's place. Jesus is God's reign, God's self-communicating love in person. At the same time, God acts in love not without humans or somehow over their heads. The coming of the reign of God is the expression of God's faithfulness as creator and covenant-initiator with humankind. Thus, God comes in a human-historical manner. In this, God does not abolish human freedom but integrates it. God indeed begins to reign there where God is acknowledged as Lord by means of faithful obedience. Thus, Jesus in his person is, both in one, God's affection for humans and their response to God. In his obedience, Jesus Christ is radically originated from God and radically surrendered to God. Christ is totally open personal existence in reception and thus is nothing before, apart from and other than this obediently accepted self-communication of God's love. He is the self-communication of God in a personal manner.

What was realized in Jesus' earthly existence became unequivocally revealed at Easter and is now expressed in the Christian confessions of faith. At the center of the Easter message stand statements of identity: The risen one is the crucified one, and the crucified one is the risen one. Also, the early Christian confessions are in their formal structure statements of identity: "Jesus is the Christ" [Mk 8:29]; "Jesus is the Lord" [Phil 2:11]; "Jesus is the Son of God" [Jn 20:31]. At first glance, it could appear as though the subject of these statements were the person of the human being Jesus of Nazareth while the title "God's Son" functions as a mere predicate. However, as we have already seen [elsewhere], confessions must be read in a reverse manner. What and who the Son of God is will be interpreted through Jesus. The substantive justification of this reversal is grounded in the Easter message which affirms that the crucified one now exists in the glory of God entirely and only because of the power of God's creative faithfulness. The identity between the crucified one and the risen one is therefore grounded not in a continuous substratum of human nature but only in God's creative faithfulness.

—JDC, 270–71

THE WORK OF JESUS CHRIST (1974)

Jesus Christ's person and work are inseparable. Jesus Christ gives himself completely to his mission; he is entirely one with it. He is the one sent and the one given for us, God's reign in love, indeed, God's self-communicating love in person. . . . Salvation is participation in God's life mediated through Jesus Christ in the Holy Spirit. . . .

The confession "Jesus is the Christ" [Mk 8:29] is a comprehensive articulation of Jesus' salvific significance. This confession says, first, that the person of Jesus himself is salvation. It expresses the uniqueness and un-exchangeable character of the Christian message of salvation. Second, this confession contains Jesus' universal and public claim and excludes thereby any false interiorizing and privatizing of the message of salvation. Third and finally, the confession articulates the manner in which Jesus is the salvation of the world. He is the one filled with the Holy Spirit, in whose fullness we participate in the Spirit. Salvation is therefore participation in God's life revealed in Jesus Christ through the Holy Spirit. . . .

As much as Jesus Christ is, on the one hand, the goal and high point of the renewing presence and action of God's Spirit, he is also, on the other hand, the entry point in the sending of the Spirit. In Jesus Christ, the Spirit has—as it were—reached its final goal, the new creation. The Spirit's further responsibility is to integrate all of the remaining reality into the reality of Christ, that is, to universalize the reality of Jesus Christ. Jesus Christ, who was conceived by the Spirit, now gives and sends the Spirit as his Spirit (Lk 24:49; Acts 2:33; Jn 15:26, 16:7, 20:22). The Spirit is now the Spirit of Jesus Christ (Rom 8:9; Phil 1:19), that is, the Spirit of the Son (Gal 4:6). It is the Spirit's responsibility to remember Christ (Jn 14:26, 16:13-14). The decisive criterion for our discernment of spirits is this: only the Spirit who is from God confesses that Jesus is the Lord [Acts 10:36]. Conversely, it is also true that no one can confess that Jesus is the Christ unless they do so in the Holy Spirit (1 Cor 12:3). Thus, the Spirit is the medium and the power in which we can have access to and experience Jesus Christ as the new Lord of the world. The Spirit is the effective presence of the exalted Lord in the church, in individual believers and in the world.   —JDC, 301–302, 306

In his effort to highlight the fullness of the mystery of Jesus Christ, Kasper unites Christology "from below" and Christology "from above" in Jesus the Christ *and also in his other Christological writings. In particular, he engages in two forms of inquiry "from below": he studies the Lord Jesus both in relation to theological anthropology and also in relation to Jesus' historical context. Further, he undertakes critical reflection "from above" as he views the Lord Jesus in relation to Triune God. In September 1979, Kasper discussed these three, "new points of departure for contemporary Christology" in lectures addressed to high school teachers. In the first selection below, Kasper undertakes Christology in relation to theological anthropology. In the second, he studies the historical figure of Jesus. And, in the third, he focuses on Jesus Christ, God's incarnate Word.*

NEW APPROACHES IN CHRISTOLOGY (1979)

Every act of human cognition in which we apprehend a specific object as finite is only possible because we somehow know infinite reality. Every finite concept exists in the horizon of an infinite pre-apprehension which we can never fully conceptualize. Every act of cognition orients us therefore to the ultimate mystery. This openness is at the same time the basis of our freedom. . . . Thus, humans are in their daily experience beings of transcendence. We experience our lives as a way into openness, as a bold venture into a dark, ultimately unfathomable mystery. . . .

What is this mystery? It is "something" different than the many not yet resolved problems with which we concern ourselves every day, problems which we shall eventually be able to solve. . . . Mystery is "something" that comprehends and makes possible everything else, that determines the whole of our existence and threatens the whole of our existence at the point of death. A human being as a whole is therefore in oneself an impenetrable mystery, a question to which the person can give no answer. According to Karl Rahner, a human being is therefore "the impoverished reference to a mystery of fullness."

We cannot deduce the Christological answer from our "human condition," our *condition humaine*. Rather, we can show how it is in this situation the meaningful and non-deduced fulfillment of the hope which is a human being. In this perspective, the Incarnation of God is "the singular highest instance of the essential realization of the human reality" (Rahner). Jesus Christ is the "symbolic reality," the *Realsymbol*, and the primordial sacrament of human existence. In Christ—as Vatican II says—God reveals what it is to be fully human [*Gaudium et Spes*, no. 22]. From Jesus Christ, the unfathomable mystery of being human becomes illuminated, above all, in suffering, guilt and death. No one can be led by deduction to this Christological answer to the question and the hope which humans not only have but actually are in themselves. All that is possible is only the proposal and the question whether in Jesus Christ there has been given what everyone is always seeking in life. The point is therefore not a deducing and demonstrating kind of discourse but an evocative, appellative and performative type of language.

—NGC, 21–22

After undertaking an anthropological form of Christology "from below," Kasper complements it as he adopts a historical–biblical mode of Christology "from below."

Biblical exegetes are successful in vividly portraying the person of Jesus, his ways of talking and interacting, thereby making him pertinent. Through their work, Jesus and his mission, the proclamation of the reign of God is again shining brightly. They are able to make clear that at the center of Christian faith is not a doctrine, a moral or even an ecclesiastical or institutional system but a concrete person with a particular name. In relation to this person we must critically assess everything that comes forth with the claim of pertaining to Christian faith. This concretely means that the Christian proclamation and Christian life must be shaped by Jesus' call to freedom; they must possess a liberating character. . . .

These general hermeneutical considerations can be strengthened by theological considerations. Faith in Jesus Christ directs itself not simply to the earthly Jesus but to the earthly Jesus who—as the risen Christ—is continually present in the church through the Holy Spirit. Faith therefore completely depends on proclaimed kerygma. We encounter the raised and exalted Jesus Christ only through the testimony of the witnesses sent by Christ. Therefore, we find in the New Testament ancient, binding confessions of faith that preceded the composition of the gospels. As a result, not only general hermeneutical considerations but also theological considerations provide a basis for generally holding that the testimony of the ecclesial community of faith is the place from which Christology and theology are only possible. Theology can critically reflect on its relation to the church, but it cannot emancipate itself from this ecclesial relationship. It corresponds to the inner, non-deducible character of the Christ event that the Christian faith is communicated to humankind, that it is witnessed to them; it is proclaimed to them with authority.

At this point, the second form of Christology "from below"— the Christology of the earthly Jesus—reaches its limits. It is at the same point where we also need to go beyond an anthropologically oriented Christology. . . .

A Christology "from below," a "bottom up" approach, can only occur in response to God's attentive care "from above." This process corresponds to the already known dialectic of human

existence. A human being is a question to which a human cannot give an answer. The answer "from above"—which cannot be
deduced "from below"—is nothing alien in relation to the "from
below" of humans. The answer "from above" is not imposed
on humans; it is nothing heteronomous. Rather, it is their inner
fulfillment. Theonomy is not heteronomy; rather, it is the basis
and fulfillment of appropriate human autonomy.

When one considers the dialectic of human existence, then
classical Christology "from above" becomes less naïve and
uncritical than it initially might have appeared. It originates even
from a sharply critical view of human existence. It respects what
Blaise Pascal called the greatness and the misery of humans.
The greatness of humans consists in their transcendent existence; they find the reason and goal of their lives only in God.
Their misery occurs because they cannot bestow this fulfillment
on themselves. The misery of being human is the impossibility
of being their own fulfillment. Human existence is given; it is
an owed existence. Humans find their salvation only in God's
self-communicating love. The unity of God and humans in the
Savior Jesus Christ cannot possibly be brought about otherwise
than "from above," that is, in the movement from God to us. In
this movement, Jesus Christ is the symbolic reality, the *Realsymbol*, the sacrament of human existence.

—NGC, 23–25

*Having started with Christology "from below" in its two
forms and reaching its limits, Kasper engages in biblically based
Christology "from above." In conclusion, he expresses his desire
that Christology strengthened the faith, hope, and love of Christian discipleship.*

Traditionally, in its biblical foundation, Christology starts with
the individual titles of Jesus Christ. That is, it usually begins with
the assumption that Jesus would have explicitly claimed to be the
Messiah/Christ, the Son of God, the servant of God, and so forth.

In contemporary exegesis . . ., this starting point has become problematic, if not impossible. Most exegetes . . . hold that these titles are not expressions of the earthly Jesus himself but are confessions of faith by the post-Easter church. In other words, these exegetes have called into question an explicit Christology by the earthly Jesus. At the same time, they maintain that Jesus proclaimed not himself but the reign of God which is the salvation of humans. Further, they have identified a much more impressive and implicit Christology by the earthly Jesus. What they mean is this: Jesus' claim [as God's Son] becomes evident indirectly through his entire manner of proclamation and his actions. Jesus proclaims not only the reign of God. In the words and deeds of Jesus, in his whole person, God is present, saving, liberating, forgiving, and reconciling. In a certain sense, one can say with Origen that Jesus is God's kingdom in person; he is the *autobasileia*.

There are different, possible ways of demonstrating Jesus' indirect Christology. We are choosing here that which is most important by proceeding from what constitutes the center and the unique mystery of Jesus' life: Jesus' relationship to "his" Father. Only when looking at it from this perspective can one appropriately understand Jesus' being-for-others, his pro-existence. Jesus' love for God as Father and his love for his neighbors as brothers and sisters belong inseparably intertwined for Jesus. For this reason, being Christian cannot be reduced either to pure interiority or to pure humanitarianism.

It is generally acknowledged that Jesus addressed God as "abba" [cf. Mk 14:36] and that the manner in which Jesus used this address represents something new in the context of the Old Testament and Judaism. In this "abba" shines forth the newness of his talk about God as a God for humans. It expresses also Jesus' own relationship with God. It is striking that Jesus used this address [to God] in an exclusive sense. He never associated himself with his disciples in this address. It is always either "my Father" or "your Father" [Mt 11:27]. It follows that even if Jesus did not apply the title Son or God's Son to himself, his

relationship to the Father is the relationship of the one and only
Son, the one who made it possible for us to be God's sons and
daughters. We have access to God as Father only in Christ and
through Christ. Only in him and through him will our neighbor
become our sibling. The Father–Son relation of Jesus does not
remain exclusive; it has saving significance for us. It is the foundation for the reconciliation of humans with God and also with
one another. . . .

This abba-relationship is the relationship of reciprocal knowledge which means the reciprocal personal union of love and
service. In this relationship, Jesus in obedience and love is simultaneously radically originating from the Father and radically
returning to the Father. Jesus Christ is nothing in himself but
is everything from the Father. He is entirely an open and empty
form for the Father. In his personal dedication, he is entirely the
presence of God's gifting and self-communicating love. Jesus'
devotion to the Father is the pre-condition for the Father's devotion to Jesus. This self-communication of the Father is not added
to the personal existence of Jesus from the outside. Rather, it
constitutes Jesus in his entire being so that Jesus' being is pure
answer, pure relation from the Father and toward the Father.
Precisely, in his personal human obedience, Jesus Christ is the
personal self-communication of God.

Out of this condensed presentation, what constitutes the center
and the unique mystery of the life of Jesus emerges. The entire
post-Easter Christology of the Son concerns nothing more than
a diligent exposition of Jesus' relationship as Son. The mutual
relationship of Jesus to the Father reveals eschatologically and
decisively who God is: God is the one who from eternity exists in
relationship of the Father with the Son; the one who from eternity
is love; the one who from eternity is oriented to human beings. . . .

This approach that starts with Jesus' abba-experience means
not only a justification of the classical Christological dogma
but also a certain correction of its one-sidedness aspects. The
personal relationship between Jesus and his Father, described in

scripture, was later rightly explicated and interpreted ontologically. The question of the relationship between the divine and
the human natures replaced the [previous talk of the] personal
relation [between the Father and the Son]. This abstract question, influenced by ancient philosophy, led to many, hardly solv-
able issues. . . .

The approach taken in analyzing Jesus' abba-experience can
substantiate not only the factual validity and the continuing
binding character of the dogmatic interpretation. It also gives
believing Christians more access to the central dogma of Christian faith. It demonstrates that Christology is not abstract speculation but catechetical inquiry for discipleship; it is not a blind
acceptance of creeds but the basis of a new way of being human,
which draws from faith in God and service to others. Theology is then immediately tied to spirituality and Christian praxis.
Christology of this kind serves as a starting point for "alternative life-styles," for which many young people are asking today:
for a life that concerns not "having" but giving, for a life in sim-
plicity, in service, for a life rooted in faith, hope and love.

—NGC, 26–29

*In the mid-twentieth century, there began a renewal in the
church's understanding of sacrament, a renewal promoted by
theologians such as Otto Semmelroth (d. 1979), Karl Rahner (d.
1984), and Edward Schillebeeckx (d. 2009). As conveyed in the
Second Vatican Councils' documents, a sacrament is "a sign and
instrument" (Lumen Gentium, no. 1); it reveals and simultaneously actualizes what it reveals. In light of Rahner's reflections
on Jesus Christ as God's primordial sacrament, Kasper advances
the understanding of Jesus Christ as the sacrament, the "sign and
instrument," of God's agape for us.*

THE SACRAMENT OF DIVINE AGAPE (1980)

In the perspective of Christian faith, Jesus Christ is the definitive
answer to the question that humans are to themselves. For Jesus

Christ as the ultimate self-revelation of God, as the image of
God (2 Cor 4:4; Col 1:15), is at the same time the fulfillment
of the human likeness of God (Gn 1:26), the new Adam (Rom
5:14; 1 Cor 15:45), in whom God has revealed humans to themselves once and for all (*Gaudium et Spes*, no. 22; *Redemptor
Hominis*, no. 10). In Christ shines forth in truth the initially only
dark and vaguely perceived mystery of being human; in him even
the enigma of pain and death becomes clear. Jesus Christ is true
God and a true human being, without confusion and without
separation [cf. Council of Chalcedon]. Thus, in Jesus Christ it
becomes evident that for humans the highest and deepest communion with God means at the same time the highest form of
freedom, individuality and fulfillment. Autonomy and theonomy
are therefore no contradiction, as secularism and also Integralism contend in their differing characterizations. God's love does
not absorb humans; rather, it accepts them and affirms them. . . .
Salvation through Jesus Christ brings about humans' communion with God and simultaneously their own freedom.

Both, communion with God and Christian freedom, can be
summed up in the word love. True love draws together and
unites; at the same time, it frees for individuality. By way of personal sacrifice, love leads to fulfillment. On the one hand, love
unites us with God, and, on the other hand, it is the concrete
realization of Christian freedom, because only the person who
is free from oneself is truly free for self-sacrifice for others. Love
of God and neighbor is therefore the fulfillment of the whole
law (Mk 12:29–31); it is the law of Christ (Gal 6:2), the new
and great commandment (Jn 13:34). In Jesus Christ, God has
demonstrated that God in God's Being is love (1 Jn 4:8, 16).

Of course, in the sentence "God is love" the hidden God is
defined by using the word love whose meaning is initially accessible through human experience. Conversely, in "God is love,"
the ambiguous and often misused word love is defined by God
as God has been revealed in Jesus Christ. This is not a run-of-
the-mill love but the love which became manifest on the cross

and is made present in the celebration of the Eucharist. This love is said to transform life and the world.

God's world-transforming love, which has been revealed in Jesus Christ, has three dimensions. First, the movement from "above" to the "bottom." It emanates from God who is transforming the matter of the world and fills it with the divine presence. Therefore, this love is neither an attaining of nor a striving for one's own fulfillment but love freely bestowed, which itself becomes self-giving love [agape].

Second, the movement from the "bottom" and "up" as response to God's love. In his sacrificial love which was fully devoted to the Father, Jesus Christ opened himself entirely to the Father's love in order to allow it to be present in freedom. Therefore, Christian love sees in adoration and self-sacrifice the perfection of human freedom.

Third, the horizontal movement. In his self-gift "for the many" (Mk 14:24), Jesus Christ established a new community. The Eucharist is the ever-present-making sign of this union; it is the covenant of love (*Sacrosanctum Concilium*, no. 47). Christian love therefore affects the service for the world and the life of the *communio*, the church. The song of love [by St. Paul] shows how little the Christian sense of love resembles the emphatic and romantic "lyric" [love] and how much it presents itself in a realistic and down-to-earth manner: "Love is patient, love is kind. It is not jealous, [love] is not pompous; it is not inflated; . . . It bears all things, believes all things, hopes all things, endures all things" (1 Cor 13:4–7).

The freeing and transforming power of this love of Christ must not be understood either in purely religious or in purely inner-worldly terms. It encompasses human existence in all of its dimensions. The Christian message relativizes and transcends the familiar dichotomies of inner and outer, personal and public-political, this-worldly and other-worldly. The love of Christ transforms one's own life and the world; it transforms joy and suffering; it even transforms guilt into a "happy fault," *felix culpa.* It transforms life in the world as much as it saves from death which it turns into a transformation to a new life. Precisely this is convincing about the Christian message, that it takes seriously the greatness and the misery of humans and thus responds to the whole [mystery] of being human. . . . Jesus Christ reveals to us humanity fulfilled by God. Jesus Christ is indeed the sacramental reality, the *Realsymbol,* both of God and also of humans. Thus, in Jesus Christ we are given the original image [*Urbild*] and the guiding image [*Leitbild*], the archetype, the paradigm for Christian and fulfilled life, for a freedom which realizes itself in love. Stated in theological terms, Jesus Christ is God's primordial sacrament for humankind.

—WKC, 32–35

GOD'S PRIMORDIAL SACRAMENT (1984)

The mystery of the kingdom of God, which is revealed to the disciples, is therefore Jesus himself as the messiah [see Mk 4:11f; Mt 13:16f]. The Pauline and deutero-Pauline language leads us to this same insight. To proclaim Christ as the crucified one (1 Cor 1:23) means for Paul to proclaim a mystery, according to some biblical texts (1 Cor 2:1). This is "God's wisdom, mysterious, hidden, which God predetermined before the ages for our glory" (1 Cor 2:7). The mystery is also God's eternal decree (Eph 1:9, 3:9; Col 1:26; Rom 16:25), which God has realized in the fullness of time in Jesus Christ in order "to unite everything that is in heaven and on earth" (Eph 1:10; Rom 16:25f). . . .

According to the Pastoral Constitution on the Church, Jesus Christ is the eschatological-definitive revelation not only of God but also of the human person. Jesus Christ, "the" image of God (2 Cor 4:4; Col 1:15; Heb 1:3), brings to fulfillment in an unsurpassable manner the divine image of all human beings (Gn 1:27). Thus, there is "revealed in the mystery of the Word become flesh the mystery of the human being." Jesus Christ as the new Adam "makes, in the revelation of the mystery of the Father and his love for human beings, human beings themselves fully known and discloses their highest calling (*Gaudium et Spes*, no. 22). As God's primordial sacrament, Jesus Christ is at the same time the primordial sacrament of the human person and humanity.

—KUS, 230–31

Since his earliest years, Cardinal Kasper has deliberately sought to develop a personal bond with the living Christ, for example, in the Mass. During his youth, he sought to meet Christ as he participated in the community of the Catholic youth association "New Germany," Neudeutschland. *As a member of* Neudeutschland, *Kasper cherished Romano Guardini's reflections on "life in Christ," which Guardini expressed in his* The Spirit of the Liturgy *(1918),* Letters from Lake Como *(1926) and* The Lord *(1937).*

FRIENDSHIP WITH CHRIST (2008)

Expensive gifts [for my First Communion] were not possible at that time. However, I received a "Schott" missal as a gift; in it, the Latin prayers at Mass were translated into German. It made me truly proud that I now could follow what was happening at the altar. My contemporaries were struck by this, and they still speak about it today. At an early age, I began—as we call it—to play the priest at Mass.

At *Neudeutschland*, the message in the Hirschberg program about the "new form of life in Christ" had a deep influence on me. —WHG, 22, 27

On the occasion of his seventy-fifth birthday, Kasper noted that we are called to become Christ's "friends" (Jn 15:15). He recalled that he was introduced to the idea of friendship with the living Christ when he as a youth participated in Neudeutschland.

Being Christian means in the end and in its depths friendship with Jesus. This Christ-centered orientation became important very early to me in the youth association *Neudeutschland* whose

Hirschberg program is centered on the message about the new form of life in Christ.

Certainly, much that one must do day-in and day-out—and sometimes this is not little—is servant work. One feels caught in a grinder, in an unmerciful calendar of appointments that others schedule for requests and responsibilities which simply come over one and from which one cannot withdraw. Unbearable, especially when one becomes somewhat older and would gladly like a bit more leisure; bearable, though, when one recalls: "This is a friend who is calling you and for whom you are to do something. He awaits you; him you should meet in the people who want you and need you."

The Johannine poem from the Heiligkreuztal Cloister in our diocese has become important to me: John rests on Jesus' chest [Jn 13:23]. In recent weeks, I have studied patristic texts which are even more profound. They say that we may quench our life's thirst at the crucified Jesus' side, pierced and opened by the lance. The blood and water which flow out are—according to the ancient church's exegesis—the sacraments of baptism and Eucharist. . . .

Friendship with Christ transforms into friendship with each other. Accordingly, one of the titles with which the early Christians addressed one another was "Friends." It appears already at the end of the Third Letter of John (1:15). Christians have to be friends, and in Christ they are indeed.   —WHG, 315–16

Shortly after his eightieth birthday, Cardinal Kasper reflected on the challenge of engaging in theology today. He culminated his thoughts in relation to the living Christ who—as Gaudium et Spes, *no. 22, states—"opened up a way" to new life.*

THE LIVING CHRIST (2013)

The truth that we as theologians have to confess and teach does not consist only in correct dogmatic formulas. Rather, it concerns a living reality: Jesus Christ is the truth in person (Jn 14:6). He is the light of the world (Jn 8:12), the light of life (Jn 1:14, 8:12). Christ is the truth that all people need in order to find the right way to live in this world's darkness, night, twilight, and fog. As theologians, we can help people so that a little more light may shine in their lives, and we can help the church to give witness so that Christ becomes the *Lumen Gentium*, the "light of the nations."

This light of truth isn't like a floodlight on an airport's runway. Instead, it is like a lantern that throws light further ahead as we go forward. This truth [about Christ] gives us sufficient light to take the next step. In this sense, after the anthropocentric turning point that has occurred in theology, we now need to undergo a theocentric turning point in theology. We have to bear witness that the joy of the Lord is our strength (Neh 8:10). Therefore, let's be joyful theologians.   —HTT, 256

3

The God of Jesus Christ

It pleased God, in his goodness and wisdom, to reveal himself and to make known the mystery of his will (see Eph 1:9), which was that people can draw near to the Father, through Christ, the Word made flesh, in the Holy Spirit, and thus become sharers in the divine nature (see Eph 2:18; 2 Pet 1:4). By this revelation, then, the invisible God (see Col 1:15; 1 Tim 1:17), from the fullness of his love, addresses men and women as his friends (see Ex 33:11; Jn 15:14-15), and lives among them (see Bar 3:38), in order to invite and receive them into his own company.

—Dei Verbum, no. 2

Walter Kasper recognizes that the Christian faith is oriented primarily to God's revelation, especially in Jesus Christ. Therefore, as Blaise Pascal observed, Christian theology concerns first of all "the God of the Bible" and only secondarily "the God of the philosophers." Although God in God's self is ontologically prior to God's self-disclosure in history, divine revelation is the starting point for our faith and knowledge of God. In particular, our inquiry into the mystery of God must begin with what the Lord Jesus has revealed about God, as passed on within the church.

GOD REVEALED IN JESUS CHRIST (1980)

In the order of being (*ratio essendi*), the Trinitarian Being of God (the immanent Trinity) precedes divine revelation (the economic Trinity). However, in the order of knowing (*ratio cognoscendi*), theological knowing begins—as in every other form of knowing—with what is visible and experienced in order to find in it evidence for the mystery of God. . . .

Christology in a historical perspective is a personal Christology. It is not, however, a personalist, narrow Christology. Rather, it presupposes a notion of person that concerns the entire human person in body and spirit as well as the concrete human existence in its physiological, biological and sociological context. The essence of personal existence is that it finds itself by losing itself and giving itself to others. A person comes to a sense of self through historical encounters [with other persons]. Persons are relations who are fulfilled in love. Persons find this freedom to love if they have experienced love from others. Only if they have been accepted as persons by others, will they enter into their freedom. In history, persons experience not only their possibilities but also their perils. They not only actualize themselves in history, they also perish in and with history. They encounter not only acceptance but also rejection and hate. Salvation is only possible if a person finds in history absolute acceptance, that is, absolute love that is stronger than death. This encounter occurs in Jesus Christ who experienced himself in his relationship with the Father in a unique, absolute and final way. Jesus Christ is the new human being who makes it possible for us to be human.

Jesus Christ not only reveals for us what it is to be human, Christ also once and for all eschatologically discloses who God is: God is self-communicating love. This understanding of God radically differs from the understanding of Aristotle for whom God is the Unmoved Mover who is sought by all who love but who in the divine essence does not love. The Greek God rules unmoved and apathetically over the terrors of history; this God is incapable of suffering. The God of Jesus Christ is the God of history who chooses to be moved by the suffering of God's creatures. This God undergoes self-emptying into history and thus enters into suffering and even death. As held by Eberhard Jüngel, God's Being is in becoming. But this becoming is different from a God who is in process. A God who is in process, who is primarily attaining self-realization in history and through history is unthinkable. If the divine becoming is understood as an expression of deficiency and incompleteness, then one must say that God cannot become, that God cannot be in process. However, there is another kind of becoming which is rooted not in deficiency but in fullness, the fullness of life and love. This is the key that is found in Jesus Christ. Because God is the inexhaustible fullness of life, God can self-empty into history and even enter into death, revealing divine omnipotence in a paradoxical form. In this self-emptying, God bursts open the shackles of death. Ever since the moment when God became fully identical with us [in Jesus Christ], there is basically no situation any longer that would be void of God or estranged from God. Because God is overflowing life and love, God can be for us life and self-communicating love.

With these statements we have reached in principle what we mean when we speak of God as Father, Son and Spirit. We mean that God in God's Being is life and love, that God is the God from eternity who can and wants to show mercy amid the groaning and waiting of God's creatures in history. The inner Trinitarian Being of God is, so to speak, the transcendent-theological condition of salvation, of the grammar of God's self-communication in history. This reality is not a matter of speculation but of the exegesis of God's self-revelation in Jesus Christ. It is the summary and epitome of the message of salvation in the New Testament.

A Christology from a historical perspective is a universal Christology. We see such a universal Christology, which understands the whole creation coming from Jesus Christ and moving toward Christ, in the New Testament, above all in the prologue to John's Gospel and also in the letters to the Ephesians and the Colossians. In the Christian tradition, this Christology was beautifully developed by Irenaeus in his theology of recapitulation. Still, a universal Christology of this kind became mostly alien to us today, for we have isolated our faith in Jesus Christ from our understanding of worldly reality. We have failed to offer people the authentic Christian perspective to understand the world and to work in it. The Christology we just described can be a help in retrieving the universal context of the Christian faith and contribute to efforts toward the de-privatizing of Christian faith.

If God in Jesus Christ is the freedom in God's self-emptying love and if Jesus Christ is, as held in scripture, the meaningful basis of all reality, then this means that the freedom that self-empties in love is the ultimate and deepest meaning of the world. Thus, love is the meaning of being. All that is finds its perfection in transcending itself, in giving itself away. In Jesus Christ and in his relationship to the Father and to us, we are given the fundamental model and paradigm of the Christian understanding of reality. A theological formulation is this: Jesus Christ is God's sacrament for the world. Christ is the universal concrete; that is, he is a concrete, unique person with a specific name, in whom and through whom there is given the world's salvation. In relinquishing ourselves in faith to Christ and becoming through Christ God's sons and daughters, we will be sent out in universal service, to a life in freedom which is perfected in love. The Trinitarian confession of faith and Christian discipleship have a great deal to do with each other. One doesn't exist without the other. Where both happen, there occurs the anticipation of eschatological fulfillment. Faith, hope and love form therefore an inseparable unity. They are the triune, fundamental principle of Christian existence. —NGC, 25, 33–35

Walter Kasper's fullest systematic presentation of the Christian understanding of God is The God of Jesus Christ *which was*

published in German in 1982. It highlights the mystery of God
for us so that we "can draw near to the Father, through Christ,
the Word made flesh, in the Holy Spirit" (Dei Verbum, *no. 2).*

THE TRIUNE GOD (1982)

Jesus' priestly prayer begins with the words: "Father, the hour
has come; glorify your Son so that the Son may glorify you"
(Jn 17:1). This prayer concerns the eschatological moment, the
inclusive and overflowing fulfillment of God's entire work of
salvation. This moment occurs in Jesus' cross and exaltation as
God's eschatological revelation. While the Father glorifies the
Son through the exaltation, the Father is also glorified by the
Son. In the glorification of the Son, the Father's own glory comes
to expression. It is this same glory which the Son has with the
Father from eternity (Jn 17:5). Therefore, this moment also concerns the eschatological revelation of the eternal essence of God,
of God's being God. It is said that God possesses the glory of
God's Being from eternity in that the Father glorifies the Son,
and the Son glorifies the Father.

People of faith are included in this eternal doxology. They
have accepted in faith and acknowledged the revelation of the
Father's glory by the Son and of the Son by the Father. Thus, the
Son is glorified in the people of faith (Jn 17:10). This glorification occurs through "another Advocate" (Jn 14:16), the Spirit of
truth. The Spirit leads the people into the whole truth. Because
the Spirit speaks nothing on its own but only what is Jesus' and
what Jesus has received from the Father, the Spirit acknowledges
the glory of the Son and the Father (Jn 16:13-15). The Spirit is
and brings about the concrete presence of the eternal doxology
of the Father and Son in the church and in the world. The Spirit
is the eschatological realization of the glory of God, the Spirit's
Being in the realm of history. This is only possible because the
Spirit proceeds from the Father (Jn 15:26) and because the Spirit
as the Spirit of truth is the revelation and brilliance, the *Doxa,*
God's eternal glory.

The genre of the Trinitarian confession is therefore not actually that of a doctrine of God. It is that of a doxology, the eschatological glorification of God. The doctrine of the Trinity is
so-to-speak only the grammar of this a doxology. In the Trinitarian confession what matters is that "all honor be to the Father
through the Son in the Holy Spirit" [Eucharistic Prayer]. This
liturgical act of praise reveals eschatologically and decisively the
eternal glory of the Father, the Son, and the Holy Spirit. The
eschatological glorification of God is at the same time the salvation and the life of the world. "And this is eternal life, that they
may know you, the only true God, and Jesus Christ whom you
have sent" (Jn 17:3). Given its use in scripture, this confession is
not abstract speculation but participation, communal life. —
GJC, 369–70

*Kasper elucidates the church's understanding of the Triune
God in relation to the church's worship in the German Bishops'
"Catholic Adult Catechism." The church's confessions of faith—
such as the Nicene Creed and the Apostles' Creed—are first of
all doxologies, statements of praise and thanksgiving to the God
who is Father and Son and Holy Spirit. In this reflection, Kasper
links our prayer to the Triune God with the strengthening of our
faith, hope, and love.*

TRINITARIAN PRAYER (1985)

Jesus did not only tell us that we have to pray as he has taught
us to pray but also that we are to pray in his name (Jn 14:13–14
and elsewhere). Therefore, in our prayer we may call on Jesus
and on the communion with Jesus and therefore be certain to
be heard. Jesus continually intercedes for us before God (Rom
8:34; Heb 7:25; 1 Jn 2:1). He has made possible for us a new
relationship to God as our Father; through the Holy Spirit we
may participate in Jesus' relationship with the Father and even
to call "Abba, dear Father" (Rom 8:15; Gal 4:6). Thus, according to the New Testament, our prayer is ultimately grounded in

the Triune God: "Give thanks always and for everything in the
name of our Lord Jesus Christ to God the Father" (Eph 5:20).
All prayers, especially in the liturgy, are oriented "in the communion of the Holy Spirit through Jesus Christ, our Lord" to God,
the almighty Father. This structure of prayer is expressed above
all at the end of the Eucharistic Prayer, summing up of the high
prayer:

> *Through him and with him and in him*
> *O God, almighty Father,*
> *in the unity of the Holy Spirit*
> *all glory and honor is yours forever and ever.*

Along with this basic Trinitarian structure of Christian prayer,
we also encounter already in the New Testament a prayer to Jesus.
The early Christian communities prayed above all, "Come, Lord
Jesus" (Rv 22:20; 1 Cor 16:22). In the Eucharistic Prayer, we
acclaim, "Lord, have mercy," *Kyrie eleison*. The church's tradition
of prayer also knows prayer for the coming of the Holy Spirit:
"Come, Holy Spirit" [hymn, *Veni Sancte Spiritus*]. And, according
to the great confession of faith, the Nicene Creed, the Holy Spirit
"is worshipped and glorified with the Father and the Son."

To the Father, we pray as God's sons and daughters; to the
Father are directed our praise and thanks, our request for forgiveness and for everything that belongs in the broadest sense of
the word to the realm of the "daily bread" [Mt 6:11].

To Jesus Christ, we pray as his disciples for everything that
is related to Jesus' cause here on earth: for the church, for our
service for the world and its people, for the mission and the
proclamation of faith. Embedded here is the New Testament's
request for Christ's return.

To the Holy Spirit, we—as the heirs of Jesus Christ—pray
that the Spirit comes, that the Spirit fills us, makes us into members of Jesus Christ, and gives us faith, hope and love, that the
Spirit gives us joy and strength, both in suffering and also in
resistance to evil.

Finally, the church will never tire in its liturgy as in its private prayer of praising and acclaiming the *Triune God*:

Glory be to the Father and to the Son and to the Holy Spirit
As in the beginning and so it is now and will be forever.

Because the confession of faith says of the Triune God "God is love," we can be certain of God's assistance in every situation because we know that nothing can separate us from God's love (Rom 8:39).

At this point, certainly many questions and issues arise. For, do we not often have the experience that it seems that God does not listen, that God is silent and not intervening? May we even hope that God would actually help us in a concrete way and listen to us? Why does God permit evil and injustice in the world? Thus, what does faith in God, the Almighty Father, and in the Father of Jesus Christ concretely mean in our lives? We must ponder now these penetrating questions by asking about the relation between God and the world and also speak about God, the Creator of heaven and earth.　　　—KAT, 89–91

In his memoir, Kasper explains that he enjoyed a sense of intimacy with God during his childhood. That is, he grew up with a sense of rootedness, of being "at home," and hence of implicitly being in harmony with self, others and the earth as well as with God. This sense of coherence was nurtured as he made pilgrimages from his village of Wäschenbeuren to the pilgrim church of the Rechberg and also to the Marian shrine at Ellwangen. Moreover, he participated in the various liturgical processions associated with the local church. Finally, as a seminarian, he was introduced to Carmelite spirituality, especially of St. John of the Cross and St. Therese of Lisieux. Today, Cardinal Kasper cherishes the occasions at his family home in Wangen with his sisters Hildegard and Inge and Inge's husband Roman.

THE LIVING GOD (2008)

[What does "home" mean?] It is a familiar land, even more, a familiar people. But it is, above all, a spiritual home, a place and room of an inner rootedness, the point of reference which remains accessible to one even if one later gets around the world. It is the place to which one gladly always again returns. Yet, it is the place to which one is always making a pilgrimage. For, even back then, it was not an ideal world, and it could not be such. In this world, we will remain pilgrims on the way. . . .

As a boy, I often made pilgrimages to the church on the Hohe Rechberg, initially with my mother and eventually on my own. Later, as bishop, I celebrated Mass there on the occasion of many Marian feast days, with many of the faithful, often outside. The place has simply grown dear to me. . . .

Being home was especially beautiful in the winter. In the evenings, the familiar songs of Advent and Christmas were sung in the family, and later, as we grew older, we joined in on the violin and the piano. The introduction into the faith and the practice of the faith happened automatically. . . .

At the seminary, the Wilhelmstift, there was daily communal prayer in the mornings, meditation and the celebration of Mass; in the evening, there was compline; on Sundays and feast days, choral prayer at St. John's Church along with vespers in the evening. The seminary rector and spiritual director conducted regular lectures in spiritual theology, to which were added days of prayer and annual retreats; of these retreats the ones conducted by Karl Rahner remain the strongest in my memory. . . .

Understandably, one could not claim that the seminary's strict schedule pleased us. But it gave us a potential spiritual orientation for eventual pastoral service, for which I am grateful. . . .

The schedule in the diaconate seminary was—from today's point of view—also strict and rigorous. At that time, it was somewhat standard. The introduction into pastoral practice included time for our engagement in the mystical tradition, especially with John of the Cross and with the "small way" of Thérèse of Lisieux. Both forms of Carmelite spirituality fit well with the spirit of the seminary building that was formerly a Carmelite cloister.   —WHG, 20, 13, 21–22, 36, 38

As Cardinal Kasper was completing ten years in the Vatican's Pontifical Council for Promoting Christian Unity and its Commission for Religious Relations with Jews, he reflected anew on the God of Jesus Christ. In this essay, he observes that when we understand that the Triune God is love itself, we experience hope even amid life's difficulties.

THE GOD OF JESUS CHRIST (2009)

God can be spoken of in numerous ways. In the course of history hardly any other word is so misused, so defiled, and so pulled into the dirt; hardly any other word is so vigorously opposed. In church piety God was often domesticated and played down. The living God who appeared to Moses in the blazing flames (Ex 3:6, 14) is hardly discernible in [talk of] a "dear God." It does not suffice therefore to speak only about vague experiences of the divine reality. It is important to speak about the God to whom the Bible witnesses: concretely, the *God of Jesus Christ*, the God who has been revealed in the countenance of Jesus Christ as the gracious God [Jn 15:13–15].

The God of the Bible is no *Deus otiosus*, no idle, indifferent God who is unmoved and uninterested, enthroned above the world and permitting it to run its course according to inflexible rules while not caring about humans and their fate. God is no emotional intuition into a vague and undefined reality. God is no faint idea of a final but ultimately ungraspable horizon in or behind all things, no irrational remainder in the face of the not abrogated contingency of existence.

The God of the Bible is the living God (Dt 5:26; Jos 3:10; Jer 10:10; Dan 6:26; Mt 16:16), the God of Abraham, Isaac and Jacob, of the living, not of the dead (Ex 3:6; Mk 12:26–27). God appears in storms and fire, however even more in the whisper of the wind and in the stillness of the heart (1 Kgs 19:11–12). In Jesus Christ, God has entered into our history, become weak human flesh (Jn 1:14), the same as us in all things except sin. God can feel with us (Heb 4:15), indeed, enduring the experience of the most profound abandonment by God (Mk 15:34). In the countenance of Jesus Christ, God shone as gracious and merciful; Jesus has revealed to us God as his and our Father. This is the God who is concerned about every hair on our heads (Mt 5:36), who goes out after the lost sheep in order to carry them (Mt 18:12-14). God goes to the cross and because of that initiates a new beginning and bestows new life. It is of this God of Jesus Christ that we as Christian theologians must speak. . . .

The essential determination of God occurs with the divine revelation of God's name in the burning bush [Ex 3:14]. It proceeds not from the identifying of the divine by the philosophers with the God of faith, but involves a clarifying, enhancing and surpassing of the philosophical understanding the divine through the biblical revelation of God. It gets serious about the fact that, unlike the philosophers' vague idea, the God of the Bible is the living, communicating and encouraging God to whom we can call and who is approachable. . . .

To conceive of God as absolute freedom means to think of God as the liberating God and the world as the realm of freedom. Theology went through a purification process after the trauma of the Thirty Years War [1618–48], marked by self-criticism and a constructive interaction with the modern Enlightenment. Today, all [mainstream] Christian churches recognize religious freedom, tolerance, independence, and respect for other religions. Without relinquishing their own identity, they seek not conflict but dialogue. (See *Nostra Aetate*; *Dignitatis Humanae*.) They acknowledge the separation of church and state and the legitimate autonomy of secular arenas of knowledge such as culture, science, economics, and politics. . . .

Today the [mainstream] Christian churches have no problem reconciling creation and evolution. Theologians of all

confessions, who stand with fundamentalist Christians and lit-
eralist atheists hold that belief in creation and evolution theories
are mutually exclusive alternatives, juxtaposing creationism and
theories of evolution. . . . Serious theology knows how to distinguish between belief that God has created the world and the
scientific question about its origin and formation.

The Triune God: An Empathetic God

With commitment for human rights, justice and solidarity, and
the preservation of creation, Christians can and should want
to collaborate with representatives of other religions and with
all people of good will. Certainly, they owe it to others to be
witnesses to the God of Jesus Christ, that is, to the Trinitarian
God who is love. This is another aspect of the talk about God
which was neglected for a long time. After many years as a kind
of "Sleeping Beauty," the doctrine of the Trinity has regained
actuality today, both in regards to historical research as well as
systematic interpretation.

Conversely, the doctrine of the Trinity does not concern arith-
metic or a kind of higher mathematics which attempts to show
how one and the same reality can simultaneously be one and
three. The Trinity can become intelligible only based on the
essence of love. Love wants to be one with the other, without
fusing with the other. Love does not absorb the other. It means
a kind of union in which the individual's identity as well as the
individuality of the other are preserved and find their ultimate
realization. Love means union while acknowledging the otherness of the other. But it does not remain a cozy tête-à-tête. It goes
beyond itself within a common third reality in which it expresses
and fully realizes itself. In this sense, the doctrine of the Trinity
is the accurate interpretation of the sentence "God is love" (1
Jn 4:8, 16). God is no solitary God. God is community in God's
Being—*koinonia, communio*—and only because of this can God
draw us into the divine community.

I can touch on this [concept] only briefly here, with the goal
of showing that the doctrine of the Trinity provides new access

to the existentially most difficult questions in theology, namely,
the theodicy issue. The question is, why is there innocent suffering? How can God, who is all-powerful and all-good allow this
to happen? Why does God not intervene? If God is good but not
all-powerful, then God is not God. If God is all-powerful but not
good, then God is an evil demon.

Of course, the doctrine of the Trinity cannot solve these questions. However, it can bring some light to the issue, and it can
help us endure the darkness of suffering and dying. It can show
that love also entails renunciation, indeed, that love and death
belong together, which is always known in great poetry. This is
also true for Trinitarian love. The divine Persons are infinite as
is everything in God. They must give one another space; at the
same time, they must relinquish themselves, so that the other
Person has space. This kenotic, self-emptying mode of existence
enables God to identify on the cross with those who are most
foreign, with sinners who deserve to die, and to enter into the
contrary of God's self, into the night of death. God can undergo
death without succumbing to it in order to overcome it and
thereby to initiate life anew. Thus, the cross is the ultimate that
God can give God's self-giving love. It is the "that than which no
greater can be thought" (*id quo maius cogitari nequit*), formulated by Anselm of Canterbury.

As such, the doctrine of the Trinity does not give a direct
answer to the question of innocent suffering. How could it?
Still, it can light a candle in the darkness and thus help us not
to lose hope in God, even in extreme need and distress. Indeed,
it can help us know that the crucified God is on our side in the
most extreme powerlessness and thus to stand firm in faith amid
all lamentations and cries "out of the depths," *de profundis* [Ps
130]. The doctrine of the Trinity is that form of monotheism
which can be existentially sustained in the face of the monstrous
scale of suffering in the world.

Yet, can God suffer? Can God suffer with us? The mainstream
of traditional theology answered in the negative. It understood

suffering as a deficiency and thus excluded the possibility of God suffering. In this regard, a change has come about in much of today's theology. Of course, if God suffers, then God suffers not in a human manner but in a divine manner. Suffering cannot be something which befalls God from the outside. God's suffering can be no passive happening and not an expression of a deficiency but only an expression of God's sovereign, free self-determination. God is not passively impacted by the suffering of creatures; rather, in freedom and out of love, the Creator chooses to take on the suffering of creation. God freely wills to be moved with compassion (Ex 34:6). Truly, God's heart turns in compassion at the sight of the misery of creation (Hos 11:8). God is not apathetic but empathetic, suffering with [others].

God does not glorify or divinize suffering. God does not simply abolish it but redeems and transforms it. Indeed, the cross is the passage to resurrection and transfiguration. The theology of the cross and kenosis, set in the horizon of the doctrine of the Trinity, becomes a theology of Easter exaltation and transfiguration. It becomes a theology of hope against all hope in the living God who brings to life (Rom 4:18). We are, as scripture says, redeemed in hope (Rom 8:20, 24; 1 Pt 1:3). The second encyclical of Pope Benedict XVI is appropriately entitled *Saved in Hope*.

God's Truth: Love as the Meaning of Existence

"God is love" ultimately means that love is the most encompassing horizon of all reality and that love is the meaning of existence. With this thesis that love is the horizon and the interpretative key for all reality, we fulfill what we had set as the challenge, namely, to understand reality in relation to God and thus to demonstrate the truth of God not in the sense of the natural sciences but to show it as rationally intelligible.

This thesis that love is the meaning of existence results in a kind of revolution in the realm of metaphysical thought. For this insight leads to the recognition that the actual and underlying reality is neither the self-existing substance nor the autonomous, modern subject. The starting point and foundational situation are much more what according to Aristotle is mere accident and the weakest existing reality: relation. The theology of the Trinity leads us therefore to a relational and personal ontology. As the relations in God ground the subsistence of the Trinitarian Persons, so by analogy in the created realm [interpersonal] relations are . . . the fundamental reality. In this perspective, humans must be understood as relational and dialogical beings. They find their fulfillment not by means of forced self-assertion but in their respectful and loving acceptance of the otherness of others. This is the fundamental paradox and dialectic of Christian existence: only by losing one's life will one find it (Mk 8:35; Jn 12:25). Not force, money, power, and influence, not self-assertion by "the fittest" but tolerance, respect, solidarity, forgiveness, goodness, and concrete love shall rule the world.

Here we can see the implications of the doctrine of God and the doctrine of the Trinity which are still not completely thought through. To think of the doctrines of God and the Trinity as the culmination of all theology presents a still not fully realized challenge, a powerful and worthwhile undertaking.

Therefore, it is time to speak about God, to witness to and to think about God. If theology wants to have an impact in the contemporary, pluralistic cacophony of opinions, then it must primarily and, above all, know what it itself is. It can only have relevance if it establishes its distinctive identity as theology, that is, as talk about God. If it does not do this, then theology and the church are reduced to ethical–moral endeavors to which over time no one wants to listen. In contrast, if theology speaks in new and fresh ways about the living, liberating God who is love, then it becomes a service to life, to freedom, justice and love, then it can serve the dignity of humans and the truth of reality. In all of the lacunae of the present time, it can open perspectives of hope. Thus, once again, one must say: it is time, it is absolutely urgent to speak about God. —EZG, 19–20, 23–25, 27–31

Two years after entering "retirement," Cardinal Kasper completed his book Mercy. *In this work, Kasper develops Thomas Aquinas's insight that divine justice realizes itself in mercy.*

THE GOD OF MERCY (2012)

The message of God's mercy is not a message of a cheap grace. God expects of us actions of righteousness and justice (Am 5:7, 24, 6:12) or—as said elsewhere—actions of righteousness and kindness (Hos 2:21, 12:2). Thus, mercy does not contradict justice. Rather, in mercy, God withholds righteous wrath; God pulls back. God does this in order to give humans an opportunity for conversion. God's mercy reprieves sinners, desiring their personal transformation. Mercy is ultimately the grace for conversion.

Let me cite just one [biblical] passage. After the people of Israel, because of their lack of faithfulness, received the justified punishment of exile, God in divine mercy gives them a new chance:

> For a brief moment I abandoned you,
> but with great tenderness I will take you back.
> In an outburst of wrath, for a moment I hid my face
> from you;
> But with enduring love I take pity on you, says the
> LORD, your redeemer.
> This is for me like the days of Noah:
> As I swore then that the waters of Noah should never
> again flood the earth,
> So I have sworn now not to be angry with you or to
> rebuke you.
> Though the mountains may fall and the hills be shaken,
> My love shall never fall away from you nor my covenant
> of peace be shaken,
> says the LORD, who has mercy on you. (Is 54:7–10)

Mercy is God's creative, imaginative justice. Although it surpasses the iron logic of guilt and punishment, it does not contradict justice but serves it. God is not bound by an alien, superior law. God is not a judge who judges according to a divine pre-determined law or, much less, as a functionary, executing the decrees of another. God possesses sovereign justice.

Thus, sovereign freedom is no capricious freedom. Nor is it an expression of a spontaneous as it were instinctive pity for the misery of God's people. Rather, it is an expression of God's faithfulness, *emet*. Already in the revelation of the divine name [Ex 3:14], there is the talk of divine favor, that is, of mercy and faithfulness. The root of the word *emet* is *aman* which means "standing firm" and "gaining hold." Thus, divine mercy exists in relation to divine faithfulness. God's covenant, once granted freely from God's bounty, is reliable; it holds and provides secure footing. Mercy is the expression of a free and gracious, inner obligation to the divine self and to the chosen people. In divine absolute freedom, God is totally reliable. We can trust God. . . .

Only if God in the divine Being is self-communicating love can God communicate outwardly to us who God already is. If God were not self-communicating in the divine Being, then the divine self-communication toward us would be an act of divine self-realization and self-development; then God would need to become through this outward self-communication of who God is. Theology would then study the divine origin, Theogony, as we find it in mythology. Further, if this were the case, then the revelation of divine mercy would no longer be a free, gracious self-bestowing but a necessary process in divine self-actualization. Only if God is love in the divine Being is the divine self-communication to us the completely free, unrequired gift of divine love.

The Trinity is the inner pre-requisite of divine mercy. Conversely, divine mercy is the self-disclosure and reflection of the divine Being. In God's mercy, there is reflected and disclosed the eternal, self-communicating love of the Father, the Son and the Holy Spirit.

We can take yet another step in order to go deeper into the mystery of divine mercy. Earlier we said that mercy is not divine self-realization but the reflection of the inner Trinitarian Being. Now we must add that God's Trinitarian Being is not self-realized in mercy. Rather, in mercy, it attains concrete expression for us and in us.   —BAR, 61–62, 98–99

In April 2013, Cardinal Kasper discussed the challenge of doing theology today and, in particular, the urgency of speaking about the God of Christian faith.

GOD FOR US (2013)

Since the council, the situation in our secularized Western world has worsened dramatically. The problem is not so much the theoretical atheism of the nineteenth century nor the so-called new atheism, which proceeds from an ideology based in evolutionary theory. Today's problem is practical atheism, that is, people's indifference to the question of God. Many people now consider the secular option to be normal.

So we should no longer worry only about the social, cultural and political effects of faith and take belief in God for granted. And, above all, we cannot engage today's new pagans with questions of internal church reform. The questions of church reform are interesting for insiders. But the people outside the church have other questions. They are asking: where do I come from, and where am I going? Why and for what purpose do I exist? How do I find happiness? Why is there evil and suffering in the world? Why must I suffer? Why do so many innocent people have to suffer, not only from unjust situations but also from natural upheavals, e.g., tsunamis, earthquakes, drought, etc.? How can a God who is almighty and all-merciful permit all of this misery? Is not belief in God, especially in the monotheistic God, the very cause of many evils such as intolerance, violence, xenophobia, and oppression?

To answer these questions we, as Christian theologians, cannot speak vaguely about a divine being or a divine dimension, as all forms of religion do more or less. Rather, we must speak of the God who in history didn't reveal something to us, but revealed and communicated to us God's very self, speaking to us "as his friends" (*Dei Verbum*, no. 2). We must talk about the God who in Jesus Christ committed the divine self to becoming "flesh" (Jn 1:14), becoming a human being who has shared our life, our joys and hopes, our anxieties and sorrows; we must discuss the God whom Jesus revealed to be God as our Father, the God for us and with us. This is the God whom the First Letter of John defined as "love" (1 Jn 4:8-16), a statement that the Christian tradition has interpreted to mean the Triune God's self-communication.   —HHT, 253–54

4

The Holy Spirit

Now, what was once preached by the Lord, or fulfilled in him for the salvation of humankind, must be proclaimed and extended to the ends of the earth (Acts 1:8), starting from Jerusalem (see Lk 24:27), so that what was accomplished for the salvation of all may, in the course of time, achieve its universal effect.

To do this, Christ sent the Holy Spirit from the Father to exercise inwardly this saving influence, and to promote the spread of the church. Without doubt, the Holy Spirit was at work in the world before Christ was glorified. On the day of Pentecost, however, he came down on the disciples that he might remain with them forever (see Jn 14:16); on that day the church was openly displayed to the crowds and the spread of the gospel among the nations, through preaching, was begun.

—Ad Gentes Divinitus, nos. 3–4

In September 1978, during the assembly of West German Catholics in Freiburg, Walter Kasper gave a public lecture on the Holy Spirit. Seventeen years earlier in August 1961, the East German government had constructed the Berlin Wall, topped with barbed wire and bordered by land mines. When Kasper spoke about the Spirit overcoming the divisions and walls between people, his audience likely thought of the Berlin Wall, running through the heart of Germany. On November 9, 1989, Kasper and his listeners may have recalled his lecture on the Spirit when the people of East Germany breached the Berlin Wall and subsequently removed it.

THE SPIRIT IN THE WORLD (1978)

Divisions are everywhere we look. Dividing lines between peoples; dividing lines between races and classes; dividing lines between poor and rich, between young and old; dividing lines between women and men, between locals and undocumented workers, people with disabilities and people with full health, peripheral groups and established associations; dividing lines between languages, cultures, world views, political parties, religions, and religious denominations. Today, it is no longer rivers, lakes and mountains that form such lines of division. With the help of technology, we have learned to overcome natural dividing lines almost effortlessly. Today, boundaries are walls with barbed wire and mine fields, walls of egoism, walls of ideologies, walls of firmly ingrained routines of thought and habits of life, walls of failure to understand each other, speechlessness, and silence. People are separated by death strips [minefields] with no path anymore on which to cross them.

Divisions create *conflicts* and therefore are dangerous. Dividing lines constrain, and, as a result, frustrations erupt in aggression. Dividing lines make people lonely, deprive them of personal relationships and empathy for one another. Dividing lines prompt anxiety about the unknown which exists behind the boundaries. Dividing lines generate feelings of powerlessness and helplessness which not infrequently lead to blind hate and irrational eruptions of violence.

Dividing lines are everywhere and with them the potential for future conflict. There is surely no lack of dynamite in our world. Therefore, the question arises: how can we breakdown these boundaries? How can we control these threatening conflicts and overcome them? . . .

In the humanism of antiquity and also Christianity there is a basic insight: humans are indeed human—and not God. *A human being as human has limits.* When humans enthrone themselves as gods, when they want to assume the role of Übermenschen, they become monsters. Humans are finite realities to whom it is granted to live only for a limited time on earth. They are certainly curious about things beyond their limits, but in this pursuit it becomes only clearer: we are reaching into an unfathomable mystery, the one from which we have come, which encompasses us, and to which we return. Humans are themselves an open question to which they themselves can give no answer.

In the language of faith, we call this mystery "God." The Bible names it, more precisely, the *"Spirit of God."* We ought not confuse the Spirit of God with our human spirit, with our ability for self-reflection and self-determination. The Spirit of God is not our interior life in contrast to our external or corporeal lives. The Bible does not know the dichotomy between spirit and body, i.e., matter, in this way. What's decisive is the distinction not between spirit and matter but between God and the world. According to the Bible, it is not only the body but also the spirit of humans that is weak, fragile flesh, which needs empowerment and inspiration from God's Spirit in order to live. The Bible tells us that the power of God's Spirit once created everything and that now the Spirit sustains and orders everything, leading everything to its goal and in this brings to fulfillment. God's Spirit is God's power of creation and history, breathing life into everything that is, so that it be. If God were to withdraw the Spirit, everything would fall back into nothingness. The Spirit of God is the *power of the future* that moves every reality to transcend itself and draws it to perfection, which it cannot attain on its own.

Therefore *we experience God's Spirit* right here in the world. There is something like a *mysticism of daily life*. We can experience God's Spirit whenever new life begins, whenever humans seek, question, hope, and pray, whenever they are creative in art and culture, whenever they strive for unity, peace and reconciliation in the world. We experience the Spirit in the sighs and groans of mistreated creatures who unceasingly hope and still constantly hit their own limits. We experience God's Spirit within our restless and tumultuous world. . . .

Whenever individual human beings are drawn together with others into the entirety of history, they may recognize everywhere in the world the signs of the Spirit who also motivates and inspires them. God's Spirit does not form narrow and fanatical minds but opens and widens our view of the world. Today we need a global, open-minded way of being Christian. Because we as Christians believe that the Spirit of God is at work everywhere, we do not need to be constantly terrified that we'll be lost and relinquish our identities when we build *bridges of dialogue* and enter into conversations with [people of] other religions and other world views. "Every truth, regardless of who attests to it, comes from the Holy Spirit" (St. Ambrose). Therefore, we may—indeed, we must—presume with confidence that God's Spirit is at work also outside our church walls; that the Spirit is also at work whenever we encounter incomplete, unintelligible and unrefined answers. We may trust the words from the unfamiliar prophets in the world and hence understand more deeply the Spirit at work among us. God's Spirit overcomes divisions as it reconciles people with one another.

Therefore, precisely for the sake of a greater unity, we must not replace discourse about God with platitudes about a better world, while we speak as though God does not exist. In order to remain non-violent, whoever strives for reconciliation and liberation among people must be a *spiritual person* who is open to the Spirit of God and draws strength from stillness, meditation and contemplation, the strength of prayer and worship.

—GSG, 442–47

On another occasion in 1978, Kasper reflected on the Holy Spirit's presence and action in our lives as God's gift and call to each of us. A fruit of the Spirit is hope. With these reflections,

Kasper elucidates Vatican II's acknowledgment that "Christ sent the Spirit from the Father to exercise inwardly this saving influence, and to promote the spread of the church" (Ad Gentes Divinitus, *no. 4).*

THE SPIRIT IN OUR LIVES (1978)

The crazy idea of being able to do and to achieve anything and everything—the idea which has cast a spell on most of us today—is actually something profoundly inhumane; it poses a cruel mental and spiritual overload. At the end of the day, no one can accomplish one's life; we shall always have the whole in fragments. Given this, the Gospel is therefore a liberating message as it frees us from the drive for achievement and perfection. The Gospel concerns not first of all the action of humans but the action of God in us. God alone can make us whole and well. This means in turn that God accepts us with all of our incompleteness. True piety is, therefore, first of all a gift and only subsequently a responsibility. It is grace, not achievement. It is existence in reception. . . .

The Holy Spirit—about which we can speak here only cautiously without being able to exhaust this mystery—is God's gracious, forgiving and reconciling outreach to humans in Person. The Spirit is in Person the gift of piety. The Spirit is the one who—according to the medieval hymn—washes what is soiled, waters what is parched, and heals what is infirmed. The Spirit warms what is frigid, melts what has hardened, and guides what is going astray. [See the hymn *Veni, Sancte Spiritus.*] . . .

The gift of the Spirit is Jesus Christ himself. In Christ, God's goodness and kindness have appeared to us in tangible form. In his words and deeds, in his life, death and his rising, it has become evident to us what the life of grace concretely means. In this way, he is the permanent basis and constant measure of all Christian piety. Scripture calls Jesus Christ "the mystery of devotion" (1 Tim 3:16). . . .

Normally, Jesus Christ meets us through our encounters with other humans and concretely through the mediation of the community of believers, the church. According to scripture, the church is the ordinary place where the Spirit is active; the church is the gift and fruit of the Spirit. . . .

In the end, the gifts of the Spirit are bestowed individually on each person. According to scripture, each of us receives a singular gift and mission in the Spirit. Therefore, the gift of piety has to be tangible in the daily life of every Christian. Indeed, there is such a thing as the mysticism of Christian daily life. Perhaps we are not much aware of this everyday mysticism. It might remain unarticulated and hidden anonymously among all of our daily experiences. But, if we become open to it, even only a little, then we shall sense also among ordinary things and events those signs which point us to the deeper and ineffable mystery of our existence; we will sense an inner encouragement to do good and warnings of evil. A person who is willing to follow this guidance of the Spirit and to surrender to it is truly pious. Scripture calls such people "children of God." Piety consists, according to theologians, in a particular sensitivity, docility and openness to the guidance of the Spirit. The Spirit can lead us on to quite unexpected and very different paths. Hence, there are numerous forms of piety according to one's talents, circumstances, gender, culture, and age. Each of us must discern one's own way. Common to all of these ways is that one must be ready to give in to the Spirit's stirring, giving it space and allowing it to work [in one's life].

A Christian life that is entrusted into the Spirit's guidance is therefore not a fixed standpoint but a way. On this way, we also have to make departures. Part of our intuition for spiritual guidance is to notice when specific devotions, which in the past were certainly correct and fruitful, have come to their end and must make room for new forms. This temporal and historical aspect is only minimally developed in our traditional forms of devotion. Quite often we have gotten solely attached to past experiences, and, in this, we have failed to be attentive to the present and the future. We became quite spiritless when we imagined how the Spirit would work [in the future]. In particular, devout or pious persons who believe in the present and future of the Spirit should have courage and trust in what's new. In this, such individuals become signs of hope for other people. Christian piety should evince not a patina of what's old-fashioned but the aura of hope.   —ZDF, 66–70

During January 1979, Walter Kasper and other theologians met in Munich in order to engage in pneumatology, that is, in critical inquiry into the mystery of the Holy Spirit. They were intent on providing a remedy for "the forgetting of the Spirit, indeed, the absence of [talk about] the Spirit in theology." At that gathering, Kasper gave an address on "a renewal of the theology of the Holy Spirit." In particular, he urged greater attentiveness to two forms of the Holy Spirit's activity in the church: the reception of church teachings and the "sense of the faithful," the sensus fidei.

THE SPIRIT IN THE CHURCH (1979)

When reflecting on the neglect of the Spirit in the church and theology, we should be aware of two teachings found in the church's older tradition: reception as an ecclesiological reality and the significance of the sense of the faithful as a criterion of dogmatic teachings. Both teachings attest in different ways that one cannot command the church from above and from the outside. Rather, the church is also gathered from below through the acts of the Spirit in the church, acts of the Spirit from beyond the church. This means that a law and even a dogma gain force in the church when they are received by the community of faith. The objective "consensus of faith," the *consensus fidei*, presupposes the faithful people's "sense of the faith," their *sensus fidei*, their Spirit-inspired judgment, their discretion, their spiritual "sixth sense." Hence, the primary responsibility of clergy is not the office of doctrine but the pastoral office of proclamation, the spiritual inspiration and motivation of the faithful. This proclamation should empower and free people of faith to become witnesses to the faith as they know it.

The relationship between these distinct gifts [i.e., the consensus of faith and the sense of the faith] is reciprocal. The tension between them is never completely resolvable. The sense of the faith is never only a passive echoing of the office of doctrine, and the office of doctrine is not simply a voicing of the majority opinion in the church. While the faith cannot be established by means of a set of official church teachings [cf. the *Enchiridion Symbolorum*], it also cannot be derived solely from a polling of the actual understanding of the faith in the church, especially since this instrument can be manipulated in our age of mass media to a degree that the Inquisition could have only dreamed. It is clear that one cannot define the church's life from a single perspective. Rather, one must approach it as an "open system" that can be studied only in a multi-dimensional set of criteria. At present, we possess such a set only in proposals and fragments. These must be developed in the context of Christology and pneumatology.   —AGP, 21–22

In 1982, Walter Kasper crafted a meditation on the Holy Spirit as the Giver of life (2 Cor 3:6). This meditation was published as a pamphlet in that year and again fourteen years later.

THE SPIRIT IN CREATION AND HISTORY (1982)

"We believe in the Holy Spirit, the Lord and the Giver of life." Thus begins the third article of the confession of faith, held in common among all major Christian churches. This confession of faith, the Nicene Creed, was promulgated by the Second Ecumenical Council of Constantinople in 381. This ancient, highly respected formulation of faith is therefore even today one of the strongest connections among the separated Christian churches. Nevertheless, as soon as we are invited to say what this statement of faith concerning the Holy Spirit specifically means, we find ourselves stammering. We are not as badly off as were the disciples of Apollos in ancient Ephesus. St. Paul asked them, "Did you receive the Holy Spirit when you became believers?" And, they answered, "No, we have not even heard that there is a Holy Spirit" (Acts 19:2). Today, most Christians say, "To be sure, we have heard of the Holy Spirit, but we have quite little awareness of the Spirit." . . . .

The question about the Spirit is often posed without an answer being in sight. The Christian message of the Holy Spirit wants to address this issue and to answer it in a surpassing manner. For it is the answer to the plight and the crisis of our epoch which—whether consciously or not—is one common cry: "Come, Creator Spirit, and renew the face of the earth!" [See *Veni, Creator Spiritus.*]

The Spirit of God as God's Power of Creation

The fundamental meaning—which underlies the Hebrew and Greek word for "Spirit"—is wind, breath, and breeze and also life and soul, since breath is the sign of life. Ultimately, these imaginative words take on the figurative meaning for "Spirit." The Spirit is the power that gives life and brings life about. It is the power which operates in everything, the power which lifts up and frees from what is customary and established, the power which creates what's extraordinary and new. The Bible proceeds from this understanding and, at the same time, criticizes and surpasses it. In the Bible, the Spirit is no impersonal, natural force; the Spirit is not a kind of principle within and belonging to humans. Rather, the Spirit is identified with life, with life that is given and empowered by God. "When you hide your face, they panic. Take away their breath, they perish and return to the dust. Send forth your spirit, they are created, and you renew the face of the earth" (Ps 104:29–30). Thus, the Spirit of God is the creative life-force in all things. At the beginning of creation, God's Spirit swept over the primal waters (Gn 1:2). "By the word of the LORD the heavens were made, and all their host by the breath of his mouth" (Ps 33:6). This Spirit of God is juxtaposed to the weakness and frailty of humans, standing apart from human power and human wisdom. It is the Spirit who creates, sustains, guides, and leads everything: "the spirit of the LORD has filled the world, and that which holds all things together knows what is said" (Wis 1:7).

The Bible's testimonies about the Spirit are not about some kind of esoteric, special knowledge or a purely interior reality. The message about God's Spirit concerns pure life per se such as the meaning of life, life's whence and whither, the power of life. Therefore, to speak of the Spirit is also to look for and to listen to the signs, for the expectations of life as well as for the futilities of life. Wherever there is true life, there God's Spirit is at work. For, as St. Ambrose said, "every truth, by whomever spoken, comes from the Holy Spirit."

The Spirit of God as God's Power in History

The Nicene Creed states that the Holy Spirit "has spoken through the prophets." Evidently, the Spirit is according to the church's creed not only God's power in creation but also God's power in history, through which God engages through words and actions in history in order to bring about through the Spirit the eschatological goal of history: "so that God may be all in all" (1 Cor 15:28).

We find time and again in sacred scripture that God calls forth humans, inspires them and empowers them to do what's extraordinary. Moses (Nm 11:25), Jos (Nm 27:18), and, above all, the judges (Jgs 3:10; 6:34)—especially the last of the judges and the first of the kings, Saul (1 Sm 10:6; 19:23)—are individuals filled by the Spirit. Beginning with David, the Spirit comes no longer erratically, unexpectedly and suddenly in occasional ecstatic and charismatic phenomena, in a sort of "happenings." Rather, the Spirit abides over David and rests on him (1 Sm 16:13). Thus, David becomes the model and archetype of messianic hope.

Above all, the coming Messiah (Is 11:2), that is, God's servant, is expected to be the bearer of the Spirit (Is 42:1).

It is the expectation of the Old Testament that at the end of time God's Spirit will transform the deserts into paradise and make them into the place of justice and righteousness (Is 32:15–18). This Spirit will awaken the dead to new life (Ez 27:1–14) and create in them a new heart (Ez 36:26–31; Ps 51:12). Finally, at the end time, there is expected a general outpouring of the Spirit "on all flesh" (Jl 2:28). It is therefore the Spirit who leads the longing creation, holding out under its groaning, to its destination, to the kingdom of the freedom of the children of God (Rom 8:19–30). This does not mean that the Spirit is at work only in the future and not already at the present time. "My spirit abides among you; do not fear" (Hg 2:5). Yet, the present actions of the Spirit are directed to the eschatological transformation and completion. It shall happen "not by might, nor by power, but by my spirit, says the LORD of hosts." As God's power in history, the Spirit effects the non-violent transformation and transfiguration of the world by changing the human heart.

The New Testament proclaims this in-breaking of the reign of freedom in Jesus Christ. All four evangelists place at the beginning of their gospels the report of Jesus' baptism by John and the descent of the Spirit on Jesus (Mk 1:9–11 and parallels). Using familiar images of that time—namely, the opening of the heavens, the sounding of God's voice and the coming of the promised Spirit—the evangelists wanted to say that with Jesus the eschatological time has begun. He is the messianic bearer of God's Spirit; he is the servant of God who does not shout and does not bluster, who does not break the bruised reed and does not extinguish the flickering wick, and who brings true justice (Is 42:2–4). Therefore, in his "inaugural statement" in Nazareth Jesus can claim to be the fulfillment of Isaiah 61:1: "The Spirit of the LORD is upon me, because he has anointed me to bring good news to the poor. He has sent me to proclaim release to the captives and recovery of sight to the blind, to let the oppressed go free, to proclaim the year of the LORD's favor" (Lk 4:18–19). Luke and Matthew go a step beyond Mark; they see Jesus as a creature of the Spirit and the Spirit's power for life, not because of his baptism but from the first moment of his existence.

The hope of the Old Testament, into which also entered the expectation of humankind, was hence fulfilled in Jesus' presence and ministry, indeed in his entire existence: the reign of God as the reign of freedom has broken in. According to the belief of the entire New Testament, it is now the task of the Spirit to make present what entered into history through Jesus' life and death, to make it universal, so to speak, and at the same time to make it indwelling in each believing Christian, giving it as one's own. Through Jesus' death on the cross and through his resurrection, the Spirit was, as it were, set free; it is now being communicated to the disciples (Jn 20:22). The book of Joel's testimony (2:28) concerning a general outpouring of the Spirit is now fulfilled (Acts 2:1–13). Paul can even say: "Now the Lord is the Spirit" (2 Cor 3:17), that is, the Spirit is the effective presence and the present effectiveness of the glorified Lord in the church and in the world. . . .

The Spirit is not so much the power of the extraordinary but the power who is able to do what's ordinary in an extraordinary manner. The Spirit manifests itself, above all, in the confession of belief in Jesus Christ (1 Cor 12:3). The Spirit is also at work in the establishment, building up, and growth of the community and in its cohesion (1 Cor 12:4–30). In individual Christians, the Spirit becomes apparent in that the believer is led not by means of "the flesh" but by the Spirit, doing the works not of the flesh but of Spirit and bringing forth the fruits of the Spirit: love, joy, peace, patience, friendliness, goodness, faithfulness, gentleness, and self-restraint (Gal 5:22–23). Thus, for one thing, the Spirit brings about the openness of human beings to God, which discloses itself above all in prayer (Rom 8:15, 26–27; Gal 4:6). Part of this openness for God is also the openness to one's neighbor, *charitas*. Love of neighbor is true Christian freedom (Gal 5:13).

The people who do what they want lack true freedom. Those who act in this way are extremely unfree because they are bound by themselves, their whims and ever-changing situations. Truly free are the people who are free from themselves, who live for God and others. The unselfishness of love is true Christian freedom in the Holy Spirit. Whenever this occurs, there is already an anticipation of the eschatological reign of freedom, in which the Spirit enables us to hope.

The Holy Spirit as Person

According to the Nicene Creed, rather than being an impersonal gift and power, God's creative, life-giving and salvific presence in the world and in the church—the Holy Spirit—is the personal giver of this gift, indeed, a divine Person. The yearning and the hope of humans, who have been created in God's image (Gn 1:27), are indeed so huge and so deep that God alone is so magnificent as to fulfill them. A person finds fulfillment only in another person. Therefore, only God's self-communication can be the ultimate fulfillment and perfection of humans and their world. This self-communication of God to humans and the world has happened once and for all in Jesus Christ. It is present time and again in the history of the church and of individual Christians through the self-communication of the God of Jesus Christ in the Holy Spirit.

Already the wisdom literature of the Old Testament came up with the understanding that wisdom is largely identical with the Spirit (Wis 1:6–7, 7:7, 22, 25), [existing] as a hypostasis [person] relatively independent of God. Post-biblical Judaism employs personal terms in reference to the Spirit: [the Spirit] speaks, cries out, admonishes, is saddened, weeps, is delighted, and consoles. It comes forth as a witness against people or as the advocate for humans before God. The New Testament uses similar kinds of expressions when it talks about the groaning of the Spirit and the Spirit's prayer in us. The Spirit intercedes for us with God (Rom 8:26); it bears witness with our spirit (Rom 8:16).

The Spirit bestows gifts as it wishes (1 Cor 12:11). All of these expressions refer to a person. In John's Gospel, the Spirit is the "Advocate" beside Jesus (Jn 14:16) and thus, by analogy to Jesus, must be understood as a person. The Spirit, from one perspective, is sent from the Father in the name of Jesus and yet, from another perspective, stands independent from the Father (1 Jn 2:1). Hence, the New Testament already gives a lot of evidence of an individuality and an understanding of the Spirit of God as a person. Accordingly, the New Testament already knows the Trinitarian formulae, of which the charge to baptize is the most widely known (Mt 28:19). . . .

The Council of Constantinople in 381, which was later called the Second Ecumenical Council, took up this issue and added these sentences to the confession of faith [by the Council of Nicaea in 325]: "We believe . . . in the Holy Spirit, the Lord and Giver of life, who proceeds from the Father, who with the Father and the Son is adored and glorified, who has spoken through the prophets." These words convey that the Holy Spirit is "Lord," which in the language of the Bible and the church Fathers means that the Spirit is of the divine essence. . . . The Spirit is not just the gift of life but rather the giver, the dispenser of life. It is not created by the Father, thus not a created being, but—according to John 15:26—goes out from the Father. Thus, we owe to the Spirit the same adoration and glorification as to the Father and the Son.

This Creed is the common foundation of all of the major churches of the East and of the West. Beginning in the sixth century, the West inserted "and the Son" (*Filioque*) after the expression "who proceeds from the Father." This Western addendum, which Rome adopted into the Creed only in the eleventh century, was one of the most significant, contentious issues in the separation between the church of the East and the West—a dispute which was not resolved until today. The Western church, of course, regards this addendum not as a substantive addition but as an interpretation which is meant to express that the Spirit is the Spirit of Jesus Christ (Rom 8:9; Phil 1:19), the Spirit of the Lord (2 Cor 3:17), and the Spirit of the Son (Gal 4:6). This Spirit is no vague spirit but must be viewed in relation to the Gospel, to the person and work of Jesus Christ, and hence the addendum must be seen from this perspective. In substance, this is also the conviction of the churches of the East. Basically, [Christians of] the East and [Christians of] the West testify to one and the same faith even though they express it by means of different conceptuality and forms of thought.

—GEI, 1–2, 6–12

Throughout his writings, Kasper explains that the church's tradition is living, that is, continually undergoing change, inspired and guided by the Holy Spirit. In this endeavor, he draws on the work of the Catholic Tübingen School and also of the teachings of the Second Vatican Council.

THE CHURCH'S LIVING TRADITION (2008)

Occasionally, the Catholic Tübingen School's theology is characterized as "liberal." On occasion, some people try to put this label even on me. This is only appropriate insofar as the Tübingen theologians have always used their own heads for their thinking and, occasionally, in the headstrong way of Swabians. The early Tübingen theologians of the nineteenth century expressed this somewhat more elegantly when they referred to themselves as "self-thinkers." For them, three characteristics of theology belong together: faithfulness to the church, scholarship and openness to the problems of the time.

Thus, the theologians of Tübingen were deeply rooted in the tradition and, at the same time, open to the new questions and challenges of their time. They understood the tradition to be the living tradition, which is only possible if it is handed on in a living manner. For this reason, conservative and progressive viewpoints are not mutually exclusive; they are not contradictory but complementary. It is always easier to adopt an extreme position since it does not need to hold together the tension between the extremes and hence does not need to find ways to reconcile—this takes work! Such a "mediation" means that theology must be [the fruit of] thinking! . . .

In doing my work on my doctoral dissertation, entitled "The Tradition of the Roman School," I realized that during the nineteenth century there were not only conflicts but also fruitful exchanges. Tübingen has remained for me a theological point of reference, though without fully defining the horizon.

—WHG, 32–33, 37–38

In his memoir, Kasper discusses how the Second Vatican Council manifests the church's living tradition.

VATICAN II IN THE LIVING TRADITION (2008)

The council was for me the fulfillment of many wishes which were in me for a long time. Later, the council's documents presented the direction for my entire development as a theologian. . . .

Today, one cannot imagine any more the interest and the enthusiasm that the council generated. Each day the newspapers were full of the controversies between the progressives and the conservatives of that time. This was thrilling and aroused interest inside and outside the church. The public discussions of the various, differing viewpoints did not harm the church; they made the church more credible. . . .

Not everything that came after the Second Vatican Council happened because of the council. Before it, the crisis was already showing itself. It would have happened anyway, and, in my judgment, it would have been much worse without the council. In a certain sense, the council established a safety-net and gave us the instruments so that we could address, in a theologically responsible and ongoing manner, the problems in and with modern society which soon posed themselves with great weight. Without the council, we would have fared poorly during 1968 [with its social and political disruptions].

To understand the council as a break from the tradition up until Vatican II, especially [a break] from the First Vatican Council, would be completely wrong and profoundly contradict the clearly expressed intention of the council itself. The Second Vatican Council was a council for the renewal of the tradition in the spirit of the early church Fathers and of the undivided church of the first millennium. The council did not throw the tradition overboard but placed it in a new light and thus opened new perspectives whose potentialities we have still not depleted fully. In this sense, the council is the foundation and beginning of a new epoch in church history and the Magna Charta for the church's way in the new century. . . .

It would be dishonest to claim that all of the liturgical movements [after Vatican II] left me cold. I could not and did not want to withdraw from what was happening, although I remained at a distance from the extremes. I struggled a bit to find the right way—my way—in this situation. This was not always easy. Yet, there were always other people and circumstances that helped me.

It helped me at the time that I resided during those years close to Münster's state hospital Marienthal for people with mental disabilities and that I celebrated Mass there every day—on week days in the small chapel and on Sundays in the large one. The Sisters were Westphalian Catholics. With them and the people with disabilities, one could not take the liberty to allow much experimentation in the liturgy; homilies had to convey "the point" in simple words. —WHG, 53, 55–56, 58–59

Kasper observes that since the church's tradition is not static but living, the church's life and the passing on of its tradition includes disagreements among its members, especially among its officials and theologians. If there were no conflicts in church, then the church would lack vitality and a future. In explaining the interplay of opposites, Gegensätze, in the church's life and tradition, Kasper is drawing on the work of the Catholic Tübingen school during the nineteenth century.

LIFE INCLUDES CONFLICT (2013)

As language is a living reality, so also tradition is a living tradition. We have the tradition that we receive only through the act of transmission, i.e., in tradition in its active sense. Tradition is not a package and a burden that we have to drag along. It is much more a fresh spring that is never exhausted. In the last analysis, tradition is always young and stays young. The church and, in a special way, theology are instrumental in translating the original sense of the Gospel into the present day. This endeavor is the very meaning of *aggiornamento*, i.e., to bring the original message, transmitted by tradition, up to date. . . .

The theologian's task of "mediation," *Vermittlung*, will often lead to conflict with current opinions. Christian faith is never obvious. We cannot avoid the scandal of the cross (1 Cor 1:23) and become everybody's darling. There can exist tensions within the church about different interpretations of the one and same Gospel. All life is constituted by tensions; where tensions end, life comes to an end. We don't want a boring, dead church but a living church. Tensions when they don't become deadly contradictions, can be enriching complementary aspects. It is in this context that I see my debate with the then-Cardinal Joseph Ratzinger. We are Catholics and remain friends. Theologians should not become stumbling blocks of division but agents of diversity within unity in synchronic and diachronic ways. As theologians, we should build up the *communio* and speak the truth in love (cf. Eph 4:15).   —HTT, 250–51

5

The Church

When Jesus, having died on the cross for humanity, rose again from the dead, he appeared as Lord, Christ, and priest established for ever (see Acts 2:36; Heb 5:6; 7:17–21), and he poured out on his disciples the Spirit promised by the Father (see Acts 2:23). Henceforward the church, equipped with the gifts of its founder and faithfully observing his precepts of charity, humility and self-denial, receives the mission of proclaiming and establishing among all peoples the kingdom of Christ and of God, and is, on earth, the seed and the beginning of that kingdom. While it slowly grows to maturity, the church longs for the completed kingdom and, with all its strength, hopes and desires to be united in glory with its king.

—*Lumen Gentium*, no. 4

Following the orientation of Tübingen's Catholic theologians, Walter Kasper has undertaken theology in the service of the church. Not surprisingly, he has given much thought over the years to the church's nature and mission. In this endeavor, he has taken his bearings from the Second Vatican Council, which, in Lumen Gentium, no. 1, characterizes the church as sacrament.

115

CHURCH AS SACRAMENT (1984)

The mystery of salvation in Jesus Christ truly enters into the world when it is adopted in faith and publicly attested. Thus, the church—the community of the believing people—is an essential moment in the realization of God's saving intention. It is, as Karl Rahner said, "the in-breaking of God's self-communication." As such, it is simultaneously the fruit of salvation and the means of salvation. It is both the actualized sign of God's salvation in Jesus Christ and also the sacramental mediation that brings this eschatological salvation to all people.

The use of the notion of sacrament in relation to the church sheds light on the relationship between the visible and invisible in the church, differing from sociology's spiritualism and naturalism. If the church is the realized sign of eschatological salvation, then this means the unity and the differentiation of the church's visible form (institution) and the content of the church's witness. It belongs to the unity of the sign and what it signifies that the actual church . . . cannot ultimately fall away from God's truth and love.   —KUS, 232–33

In speaking of the church, the Second Vatican Council acknowledges that the church is a mystery, a complex reality that we can increasingly understand but never fully fathom (see Lumen Gentium, *no. 5). Similarly, in the German bishops' "Catholic Adult Catechism," Kasper discusses the church as mystery.*

CHURCH AS MYSTERY (1985)

The church is a truly human entity, and, at the same time, the church is more than one can see and grasp. One can understand the church appropriately only in the *perspective of faith*. For ultimately the reality of the church is rooted in the salvific decree of God the Father and in the salvific action performed through Jesus Christ in the Holy Spirit. For this reason, the church is *one complex reality*. On the one hand, it is the visible, earthly church which needs legal processes and structures for the realization of its mission. It is established and directed in this world as a society, and it is realized and ordered in the Catholic Church, which is led by the successor of Peter and the bishops in community with this successor. On the other hand, the church is a spiritual reality—that is, a reality filled by the Spirit of Christ, which can be apprehended fully only in faith (*Lumen Gentium*, no. 8). In it, the saving mystery of God, which has come into the world once and for all in Jesus Christ, is continually present in history in a concrete way (Eph 3:3–12; Col 1:26–27).

In order to express both dimensions of the church, the Second Vatican Council teaches that the church is in Jesus Christ the sacrament, that is, "a sign and instrument" of the universal salvation of the human family (*Lumen Gentium*, no. 1; *Gaudium et Spes*, no. 42, 45; *Ad Gentes*, no. 1). What's visible is therefore essential to the church; however, it is only a sign and instrument of the church's spiritual dimension. Therefore, a twofold statement is made: the church is an instrument for the realizing and passing on salvation. However, it cannot be defined any more only in terms of its function. The church is more! Being a sign that makes salvation present, it is at the same time the fruit of salvation. It is the public manifestation of the mystery of salvation in the world. —KAT, 271

When Walter Kasper became the bishop of Rottenburg–Stuttgart (June 17, 1989), he chose his episcopal dedication from Ephesians 4:15, "living the truth in love, we should grow in every way into him who is the head, Christ." At the Mass of his episcopal consecration, he preached on the dedication itself: "Living the Truth in Love." As the excerpts below convey, he spoke about truth in relation to Jesus Christ and the church. In doing so, he highlighted faith, hope and love in the Christian life.

LIVING TRUTH IN LOVE (1989)

Grace and peace of God, our Father, and of the Lord Jesus Christ be with you! With this greeting of the apostles, I cordially welcome you here in the cathedral and in the entire diocese today, on the day of my episcopal consecration. . . .

My dear sisters and brothers, if we hope not merely to survive but to live truly human lives, then we need not only clean air and green trees, though we surely need these. Our souls also want to breathe in healthy ways. We can live human lives only if we hold ourselves to the truth in love.

The truth, this means not only true statements. The truth is the true reality on which one builds and in which one can trust in life as well as in death. The truth of our lives is God's unbreakable faithfulness, God's unconditioned yes to each one of us and to all of us as God's people. God has spoken this yes in Jesus Christ once and for all. Christ is "the way, the truth and the life" (Jn 14:6). He is the key, the center, and the goal of the entire history of the human family, the Alpha and the Omega (Rv 1:8). He is the salvation of the world, he alone. He, Jesus Christ, is therefore our program; he is our leader in the faith (Heb 12:2).

The active handing on of faith in Jesus Christ is *the* duty, my primary duty as bishop. This duty rests on all of you as well. . . . The Gospel without additions, however also without reductions, is the most important investment that we could carry into the future. For the truth sets us free (Jn 8:32) from quickly changing voices and trends. It gives stability and substance to our life. It grounds hope.

You will ask, how do we do this? I have no ready-to-go solutions to offer you. However, I can pass on to you the answer of the apostles: "Living the truth in love" (Eph 4:15). For the truth of Jesus Christ (Jn 3:21) has to be done. God's Word has become flesh, and it wants to be concretely "located" in the flesh with our world: in our families, places of work, in our leisure time. Jesus Christ concretely encounters us in the people who are sick, disabled, poor, and suffering in all forms (Mt 25). Not least is Christ actively present in the church, which is his body, formed in love (Eph 4:16). The church is the house of truth, God's sign in the world.

I know that the word "church" does not taste good today to many people. They cannot even hear it any more without reacting scornfully or even bitterly. They even think the church is already in a coma. I also know about the need for a renewal of our church, and I will remember this in my new office. Nevertheless, I oppose all complaints from the left and also from the right. For I also know of the beauty of the church, the depth of its faith, the richness of its liturgy, and the fruitfulness of its service. I love *this* church. . . .

The church is a grand, world-encompassing, truly catholic community of sisters and brothers of all peoples, languages, cultures, and skin colors. I greet therefore most cordially Christians from other lands who reside among us. I also warmly greet those to whom we are bound on the basis of our common baptism, even if we are unfortunately not yet in full communion with one another. I greet our Orthodox Christians, Protestant Christians and Old-Catholic Christians. I am delighted that they are celebrating here with us.

My shepherd's staff shall tangibly express what truth in love means. Firstly, it points to the past, to the tradition. Tradition is not dead ballast but a rich heritage which we must re-discover as emergency rations for a difficult stretch on the way.

This staff also points upward. God alone can kindle new embers of faith; God must bestow on us the handing on of the faith. For this, we can only pray. Only the way of change, the way to the past and the way upward show us in a correct manner the way into the future. We want no restauration; we want to build a church for tomorrow, for the third millennium. This is only possible if our faith is expressed not only in documents, structures and institutions—as important as these are—but if it is rooted above all in our hearts.

Thus, the shepherd's staff finally points within. There, a bud is sprouting. It recalls the signet of our diocesan synod. Out of the seemingly dead root, a rose blooms (see Is 11:1). As the staff of Aaron blossomed overnight (Nm 17:23), so our church—and

of this I'm convinced—is emerging, after a cold winter, into a
new spring.
Help with this! Let us pray together. Pray for this! Let us
stand together! The grace of God, the peace and the joy of our
Lord Jesus Christ and the communion of the Holy Spirit be with
us. Amen.   —WAH, 36–37

*In his memoir, Kasper recalls the form of Catholicism during
his childhood and youth. During Kasper's first twelve years,
the Catholic Church—especially in his diocese of Rottenburg–
Stuttgart—stood as a bulwark against Adolf Hitler's National
Socialism. Among the church's outspoken critics of Nazism was
the diocese's Bishop Johann Baptist Sproll who, beginning in
the 1920s, often preached against Nazi ideology and actions.
In 1938, Sproll had to flee the diocese of Rottenburg–Stuttgart
and go into hiding because he publicly opposed Hitler's "annex-
ation" of Austria. In June 1945, Sproll returned to his diocese
and helped the people recover from their years of Nazi tyranny
and war. In the war's aftermath, the diocese promoted youth
groups such as the "Swabian Catholic Youth Association" and
the "New Germany Association"/"Neudeutschland." As a member of these youth groups, Kasper met Bishop Sproll (d. 1949)
and also his successor Bishop Carl Joseph Leiprecht (d. 1975).
During a youth trip to Rome, he met Pope Pius XII (Eugenio
Pacelli).*

CHURCH AS COMMUNITY (2008)

I met Bishop Sproll for the first and last time in [my village of]
Wangen. He was seriously ill and had to be carried into the
church because he could no longer walk. At that time, I was a
member of the "Swabian Youth Association" and had the honor
of holding our banner. Thus, I stood at the front of the church's
choir. His visit was deeply moving for everyone, especially since
he sought reconciliation with everyone, even with his personal
opponents of that time. . . .

We were not necessarily more devout than today's youth, well, perhaps a little bit. However, it was important that we spent time with our close friends before and after these meetings. The "Compline" [evening prayer] was basically a gathering at which the priest-vicar—who could play soccer very well—wasn't missing. This church community was thus a comrade-friendly assembly of like-minded youth. . . .

I still remember when I gave my first presentation in front of a bishop. [It was Bishop Carl Joseph Leiprecht who came to celebrate Mass with the youth during the *Neudeutschland* camp in Leutkirch.] Back then, we were not as well versed in public speaking as the young people are today. In the following years, I often wrote him, asking him if he could kindly support our camps and trips. And when he sent us 100 Marks, it was a lot of money in those days. During that time, there grew a bond of trust with this bishop who would later ordain me to the priesthood and to whom I was honored to offer advice on some occasions when I was a professor. . . .

In 1952, I visited Rome. The city—which was influenced by antiquity, early Christianity, Renaissance, and Baroque with its grand basilicas and catacombs—was an overwhelming experience. . . . To be sure, I vividly remember the first papal audience of my life. For us, Pius XII was a sacrosanct authority who was honored. We would never have thought of criticizing him. Especially among us in Germany, he was highly respected.

The critique for his stance during [the Holocaust] was not coming from those best informed contemporary witnesses [including surviving Jews] but only later, particularly when Rolf Hochhuth published his problematic work *The Deputy* in 1953 and thereby influenced public opinion.

When I entered the seminary, there were seventy of us. This unbelievable number of seminarians reflects a moment in the church which is very different from ours today. During the 1950s, after the collapse of the Third Reich and the horrors of the war, there was not only a religious hunger but also a spirit of optimism of being able to rebuild a Europe based on Christian polity. . . .

My ordination was a blessed day for my parents, my siblings and me. Not only did a long-cherished wish come to true; ordination is both a gift and a mission. I dedicated it to words in 2 Corinthians 1:24: "We are not masters of your faith but servants of your joy." . . .

In 1957–58, during the first years of parish ministry, I had to hear confessions for many hours on Saturdays and also before the major feast days. On Sundays, one had to preach often at four Masses. In the evenings during the week, we had to visit those who had moved to the area [which were many, coming from eastern parts of Germany and Poland]. If you like, you can call this a crash course in life experience for a twenty-four-year-old parish priest.

Already then, it was apparent to me that the times had changed. Church attendance dropped. The number of children and teenagers in the parishes became lower. In the schools were the first problems. The crisis did not start after the Second Vatican Council, it was evident already long before.

The last years of Pius XII's pontificate were marked by a certain rigidity. When he died, all of a sudden there came to the fore pent up questions which had been previously discussed only in the smallest circles. . . .

What happened after the council was already, albeit unconsciously, prepared for in our minds, although we had not fully formulated it. In Tübingen, we were taught to understand the life and teachings of the church in and through their historical context. I remember when I bought the first volume of *Theological Investigations* (1954) by Karl Rahner, S.J. I was totally fascinated and began to read his essay on the development of doctrine while I was still walking on the street. It clearly expressed so much of what I was intuitively searching for but was unable to articulate.

A similar breakthrough was *Lay People in the Church* (1953) by Yves Congar, O.P. I had met him already years earlier in Tübingen at a Sunday morning lecture in the main auditorium. I took notice of this latest French theology [the *nouvelle theologie*]; beside Congar, there was particularly Henri de Lubac, S.J. For a long time, they were under suspicion and censure. Now, they were—first *de facto* and later officially—rehabilitated and, within a few months, were regarded as authorities.

Also, Cardinal Augustine Bea—who was charged by Pope John XXIII with chairing the newly founded Secretariat for Promoting Christian Unity, today called the Pontifical Council for Promoting Christian Unity—also came to Tübingen during the preparation period for the council. In the university's ceremonial hall, he delivered a lecture on the unity of the church. I could not have even imagined that I would one day become his successor [as the president of the Pontifical Council for Promoting Christian Unity].   —WHG, 25, 26, 27, 28–29, 36, 38–39, 39–41, 42–43

As a theologian in Tübingen, Kasper participated in the West German Catholic Church's national synod in Würzburg (1972–75) and also in the synod of the Diocese of Rottenburg (1985–86). In 1985, he served as the theological secretary for Pope John Paul II's Extraordinary Synod of Bishops in Rome. Based on these experiences, as well as on his study of church history, he holds that church governance on all levels should include synods. In his memoir, he discusses the importance of synods in the church's life.

THE VALUE OF SYNODS (2008)

It would not be an innovation if synods were held, on a regular basis, in a local church or a church region. In support of this practice, one could appeal to the church's oldest traditions. We find synods in the East already in the first centuries and also later in Rome as well as in Africa and France. Boniface revived the habit of holding synods. In the Middle Ages, provincial synods were important for the church's renewal. This is true, too, for the diocesan synods which were held after the Council of Trent and contributed essential elements to the Catholic renewal. One need to think only of the synods which the saintly Bishop Charles Borromeo held in Milan and which were studied extensively by Angelo Guiseppe Roncalli who became Pope John XXIII.

After all, important ecumenical arguments speak for the revival of the church's synodal structure. To be sure, synods as they have developed in the Protestant churches during the twentieth century cannot be a direct model for us, since they reflect a different approach to the office of the bishop. In comparison, synodality as practiced in the East is closer to our understanding. The renewal of our own tradition of synods would surely benefit the convergence of the East and the West.

—WHG, 74

As the theological secretary for the Extraordinary Synod of Bishops, Kasper gave much thought to the church's nature and mission. He sought to elucidate Vatican II's assertion that "the church longs for the completed kingdom and, with all its strength, hopes and desires to be united in glory with its king" (Lumen Gentium, *no. 4*).

This position [of theological secretary] led me for the first time into the world of the Vatican and the global episcopacy. Well, at first it brought me a lot of work. In preparation, I had not only to study piles of position papers by the world episcopacy. I also once again read closely all of the documents of Vatican II. This led me to the insight that *communio,* "community"—specifically, the understanding of the church as *communio*—is the fundamental idea of the council.

I was able to introduce these thoughts into the synod's deliberations and its concluding document. This meant an important step in the reception of the council. While until then the image of the "people of God" stood at the center, now the *communio* ecclesiology came to be more and more valued in theology and in statements concerning doctrine.

In post–Vatican II discussions, the image of the "people of God" had often become detached from its context in salvation history. It no longer had the sense of the Greek *laos*, "chosen people of God," but was derived from the political concept of *demos*, "people." From that point of view, the understanding of the church as a democracy was not too far-fetched.

The notion of *communio*, in Greek *koinonia*, includes in itself the appropriate elements of the people-of-God ecclesiology but at the same time stresses that the church lives not "from below" but "from above." It lives not from the people, also not from the hierarchy, but out of God's Word and the sacraments, especially the Eucharist. —WHG, 97–98

During his last year as the bishop of Rottenburg–Stuttgart, Kasper wrote an essay, entitled "Toward the Theology and Praxis of the Episcopal Office," in which he calls for the retrieval of the balance or complementarity in ecclesial governance between the "universal church" and the "local churches." Arguing for a greater recognition of the authority of bishops and conferences of bishops, he criticizes the emphasis on centralized ecclesiastical authority in the document "Concerning Some Aspects of the Church as Communio," issued in 1992 by Cardinal Joseph Ratzinger as the Prefect of the Congregation for the Doctrine of the Faith. This essay was included in a Festschrift for Bishop Josef Homeyer, Auf neue Art Kirche sein. It was published in 1999 as Kasper was getting settled in Rome and beginning to work as the theological secretary for the Pontifical Council for Promoting Christian Unity and also for the Commission for Religious Relations with Jews. In February 2000, Kasper attended a Vatican symposium at which Cardinal Ratzinger gave a lecture in which he sharply criticized Kasper's recent essay on ecclesiology. In his memoir, Kasper recalls that symposium and its aftermath.

DIFFERING THEOLOGIES OF
THE LOCAL CHURCH (2008)

I had been in Rome for just half a year and hardly knew anyone. On February 27, 2000, I was for the first time at a symposium in which most of the cardinals and bishops of the Roman Curia were participating. Its topic was the thirty-fifth anniversary of Vatican II's Dogmatic Constitution on the Church, *Lumen Gentium*. Cardinal Ratzinger gave a brilliant lecture on the mystery of the church. A third of the lecture critically took issue with my position in the cited essay, explicitly mentioning my name. I found myself in a difficult situation. This was not the reception into the Roman Curia that I had wished for.

Pope John Paul II helped me psychologically. Arriving after Ratzinger's lecture, he came to me, sitting in the front row. Without knowing about the lecture or even mentioning it, he jokingly called me *Homo sinaiticus* because, just before the symposium, I had joined him on his anniversary pilgrimage to Mount Sinai. His gesture was balm for my soul.   —WHG, 151

Cardinal Kasper initially chose to avoid a public disagreement with Cardinal Ratzinger. But when he learned that Ratzinger's lecture had subsequently appeared in three widely circulated journals, he realized that he needed to clarify his position which had been inadequately presented in Ratzinger's lecture. For this reason, Kasper published an essay in the journal Stimmen der Zeit *(December 2000), which led to public statement by Ratzinger and a further response by Kasper. Amid this public theological disagreement, Pope John Paul II made Kasper a cardinal (February 21, 2001) and appointed him to lead the Pontifical Council for Promoting Christian Unity and also the Commission for Religious Relations with the Jews. In his memoir, Kasper comments on his theological disagreement with Cardinal Ratzinger concerning the issue of the theological status of local churches.*

People still go back to this essay and ask me about it. This is a sign that it treated not only a theoretical problem but also one which is absolutely pertinent in practical matters and in church polity and which is worth still further reflection. The council charged us with this issue and, I believe, it has not yet been talked through fully. I, too, have sought to think more about it and came to the point of speaking of the one church of Jesus Christ and the individual churches. That the church is the *ecclesia una*, the "one church," is clearly expressed in the profession of faith. It remains to clarify this issue: that—and how—the many individual churches are not just a part and province of the one church and further that the one church is concretely present in them. It is present in such a way that if they were to isolate themselves, they would be injured and wounded in their most fundamental ecclesial essence. —WHG, 153

Kasper holds that the theological authority of the local churches is significant because the church's new evangelization can only succeed if it arises from the local churches themselves.

Mission is the alpha and omega of being church. The church is missionary in its nature; this is stated in all of the texts of Vatican II. This pertains not only to the mission to foreign lands but also at home.

In order to be more missionary there should be more religious zeal, more confidence. Much too often we trust in modern methods. Although helpful, only an authentically lived faith can electrify and catch on. . . .

The new evangelization cannot occur any differently than the first. It spread out from spiritual centers, at that time mostly cloisters. Today, these can be vibrant parochial centers. To create spiritual centers that shine forth seems to me to be the order of the day. —WHG, 155–56

Over the years, Walter Kasper and Joseph Ratzinger sustained good will between them, even amid their theological

*disagreements. From the start of Benedict XVI's papacy on April
19, 2005, Cardinal Kasper resolved to support and assist the
new pope as much as possible. In his memoir, he recalls that he
said to himself:*

This is no longer Joseph Ratzinger whom you have known
for forty years and with whom you have occasionally crossed
swords. This is Benedict XVI who, as a matter of course, is to be
met with full loyalty.   —WHG, 135

*In 2008, on the occasion of Walter Kasper's seventy-fifth
birthday, Pope Benedict XVI sent the cardinal a letter with these
words of praise and graitude:*

POPE BENEDICT'S PRAISE OF
CARDINAL KASPER (2008)

Almost a half of century has passed since we met at the University of Münster in the early 1960s. . . . After a moment of radiant promise, being Christian became again tedious. We are still
in a state of wrestling, although it is a state of hope, pregnant
with a sense of departure. A new form of Christian existence is
emerging. Once more we see that the church opens up the future
precisely because its perspective is beyond the temporal realm
and helps in comprehending time from the stance of eternity. In
this difficult process, you were always in the forefront. During
those years, you had the courage to take up the central themes
of theology and to interpret them anew. Your Christology, a new
edition has just appeared, is an orientation for many people,
including theologians and non-scholars, in various languages
and cultures. . . . Your book about God is no less important. You
have reminded us again of the true center of theology which in
its essence is talk about God; it is nourished by God's words to
us, and it leads into conversation with God. . . . In conclusion, it
remains for me cordially to thank you for everything that I have

learned from you and for our collaboration over many years, during which, although we were not always in agreement, we knew that we were walking together in the service of Christ and the church.

—Benedict XVI, "Geleitwort," in *Gott Denken und Bezeugen*, ed. George Augustin and Klaus Krämer (Freiburg: HV, 2008), 10

One year after his retirement from the Vatican's offices for ecumenism and Jewish relations, Cardinal Kasper published the book on ecclesiology that he had intended to write before he became a bishop, The Catholic Church: Nature, Reality and Mission. *In it, he includes his theological reflections on the relationship between the universal church and the local churches.*

THE CHURCH: UNIVERSAL AND LOCAL (2011)

The issue of papal primacy as well as the issue of collegiality and synodality lead to the question of the relationship of the universal church to the many, local or individual churches. In the New Testament, the term church, *ecclesia*, is used in the singular and also in the plural, referring to several local churches. According to the understanding of the New Testament, the one church is present in each particular church. Paul speaks of the "church of God which is in Corinth" (1 Cor 1:2; 2 Cor 1:1). Similar expressions are found in the writings of the early church Fathers. Thus, it is absolutely evident that in each particular church, which celebrates the Eucharist, there is present not just a part but the one church of Jesus Christ.

Therefore, since there is the one church which is present in the many local or particular churches, no particular church can isolate itself from the one church. Each local church is rather a concrete expression of the one church and depends on the communion of all other local churches. There are many churches, and nevertheless they are all the one church not because of a subsequent federation but because of their very being. As such, they grant one another peace, *pax*, characterizing themselves as

a solidarity and offering each other hospitality. First and foremost, they agree in the one, handed-on doctrine of the faith.
Above all, Cyprian of Carthage emphasized the unity and indi-
visibility of the episcopacy. In the eastern churches, Basil often
invoked in his letters the necessity of the unity and collaboration
among the churches of the East and West. . . .

The perichoretical unity of the universal and individual churches
beyond centralism and federalism is something unparalleled in
secular structures. Since the church is a divine–human reality
though, it must be permitted to ask what practical consequences
this might have. In its praxis, for example in its canons regarding
episcopal appointments, the early church must respect both universal–ecclesial and local–ecclesial aspects, always wrestling for
the right balance between unity and legitimate plurality. It should
not impose burdens beyond the necessary ones (Acts 15:28). It is
evident that this principle is ecumenically significant, particularly
in relation to the churches of the East.

Every centralism involves the danger of changing to the contrary, sooner or later. For the situation and the challenges in the
world, despite all globalization, differ so much that it is increasingly impossible to govern everything in a centralized way. If it
is attempted nevertheless, then the centralism will become difficult to bear after a while. It will provoke increasing disgrun-
tlement, and in practice it will sooner or later quietly lead to an
inner renunciation of unity. In contrast, a prudent balancing of
unity and diversity could overcome built up discontent and distrust.   —KAK, 387–88, 391–92

Kasper concludes The Catholic Church *with his characteristic
emphasis on hope nurtured by the Holy Spirit.*

HOPE IN A NEW PENTECOST (2011)

One cannot determine the renewal of the church by means of a
sophisticated program. Ultimately, the renewal is possible only
through a renewed Pentecost of which the blessed Pope John

XXIII spoke when he convoked and subsequently opened the Second Vatican Council on October 11, 1962. If we are convinced that in the end only the Spirit of Pentecost can bestow renewal, then above all we must do what the first disciples did before Pentecost. At that time, the apostles and the women, who had accompanied Jesus, had gathered, along with Mary the mother of Jesus, and waited in prayer (Acts 1:12–14). In the same way, the church's future is determined today first of all by prayer, and the church of the future will be first of all a church of prayerful people. —KAK, 487–88

In his book Mercy, *Cardinal Kasper illumines an eclipsed aspect of the church as he reflects on the mystery of divine mercy. In doing so, he concludes with an allusion to his episcopal motto, "Truth in Love" (Eph 4:15).*

CHURCH: SACRAMENT OF MERCY (2012)

The commandment of mercy is given not only to the individual Christian but also to the church as a whole. As for the individual Christian and also for the church, the precept of mercy is grounded in the church being the Body of Christ. For this reason, the church is not a kind of social-service agency; as the Body of Christ, it is sacrament of the abiding, effective presence of Christ in the world; as such, it is the sacrament of mercy. It is this as the *Christus totus*, Christ's head and members. Thus it encounters the Christ in its own members and in people in need. Through word and sacrament as well as through its entire life in history and through the life of the individual Christian, it has to make present the Gospel of mercy which is the person of Jesus Christ. The church itself is, however, also the object of the mercy of God. As the Body of Christ, it is rescued by Christ, holding in its bosom also sinners, and must therefore be purified again and again in order to be pure and holy (Eph 5:23, 26). Hence, it must continually ask itself if it is indeed living up to its calling. Conversely, we—like Jesus Christ—ought not to be self-righteous but merciful in dealing with the idiosyncrasies and flaws of the church. In this regard, we must be clear: a church without *charitas* and without mercy would no longer be the church of Jesus Christ. . . .

Therefore, the message of mercy has consequences not only for the life of the individual Christian but also far-reaching consequences for the doctrine, life and mission of the church. The worst reproach which the church can receive and which it actually often receives is that it itself does not do what it proclaims, indeed that it is experienced by many people as unmerciful and rigid. On this point, Pope John XXIII said at the opening of the Second Vatican Council that above all the church today must employ the instruments of mercy. In his encyclical "On the Mercy of God," Pope John Paul II took up this message and dedicated an entire chapter to "The Mercy of God in the Mission of the Church." He underlined that the church's mission to bear witness to the mercy of God. . . .

It is easy to misunderstand and to misuse the word mercy not only in regard to our personal lives but also the institutional realm of the church. This happens in both areas if one confuses it with laxity and a laissez-faire perspective. Whenever that happens, the adage pertains to *orruption optimi pessima*, "the downfall of the best is the worst." There exists then the danger that God's dearly "bought" grace, "earned" on the cross with God's own blood will be turned into a cheap grace, a grace always on sale. Dietrich Bonhoeffer expressed this thought without any ambiguity: "Cheap grace means justification of the sins but not of the sinner." "Cheap grace is the preaching of forgiveness without penance, baptism without community-discipline, the Lord's Supper without the confession of sins, absolution without individual confession."

The general failure of church discipline is one of the weaknesses in the contemporary church and a misunderstanding of what mercy means in the New Testament and the pastoral dimensions of the church. The de-construction of a rigid legalistic praxis without the simultaneous construct of a Gospel-shaped, new praxis of church discipline has led to a vacuum, which has allowed scandals leading to a serious crisis in the church.

Since church discipline is based on the Gospel, we remember the need for a church discipline in the spirit of the Gospel. Paul makes clear that excommunication is to be understood as a restorative punishment; it should bring sinners to their senses and trigger a personal transformation. Paul wants "to deliver" the sinner "to Satan . . . so that his spirit may be saved on the day of the Lord" (1 Cor 5:5). When the sinner repents and undergoes a personal transformation, the community shall exercise clemency (2 Cor 2:5–11). Punishment is therefore the last option and as such temporally limited. It is the last drastic act of mercy. One can speak of an instructive and medicinal significance to the discipline of penance. Ultimately it has eschatological significance; it anticipates eschatological judgement. The temporal punishment guards against eternal punishment. Thus understood, it is not as unmerciful harshness but as an act of mercy.

Such an understanding of church discipline as the bitter but necessary medicine of mercy is neither legalism nor laxity. It corresponds to a tradition which—understanding Jesus Christ, in light of his healing miracles, to be doctor, savior, healer, medic— reveres the holy doctors (Luke, Cosmas, Damian and others) and understands the pastoral minister, especially the confessor, to be not only a judge but above all a healer of souls.

This medicinal understanding of church law and church discipline leads us to the fundamental question concerning the interpretation of church law, thus to the hermeneutics of church law. This is a wide area which we cannot treat comprehensively here but only from the perspective of the relationship between church law and mercy. . . .

Theologically, the point is to do truth in love (Eph 4:15), hence, doing what is just, guided by love. Thus ecclesiastical judges need not only sound human judgment but also the call to be just and merciful judges after the example of Jesus. . . . They should take their bearings from the merciful judge, Jesus Christ. The kindness and goodness (*epikeia*) of Jesus Christ ought to serve as the rule.   —BAR, 155, 157, 171–74, 176–77

6

Ecumenism and Jewish–Christian Relations

Today in many parts of the world, under the influence of the Holy Spirit, many efforts are being made in prayer, word and action to attain that fullness of unity which Jesus Christ desires. This sacred council, therefore, exhorts all the catholic faithful to recognize the signs of the times and to take an active and intelligent part in the work of ecumenism.

—*Unitatis Redintegratio*, no. 4

Sounding the depths of the mystery which is the church, this sacred council remembers the spiritual ties which link the people of the new covenant to the stock of Abraham.... [T]he apostle Paul maintains that the Jews remain very dear to God, for the sake of the patriarchs, since God does not take back the gifts he bestowed or the choice he made. Together with the prophets and the same apostle, the church awaits the day, known to God alone, when all peoples will call on God with one voice and "serve him shoulder to shoulder" (Soph 3:9; see Is 66:23; Ps 65:4; Rom 11:11–32).

—*Nostra Aetate*, no. 4

*As Walter Kasper has engaged in ecumenism and Jewish–
Christian dialogue, he has remained anchored in the Christian
belief that Jesus Christ is "the key, the center and purpose of the
whole of human history" (Gaudium et Spes, no. 10)—the belief,
evident in the text below, that he articulated at the start of his
theological writings. Yet, also since the outset, he has simultaneously conveyed respect for others' religious convictions and religious communities. Kasper recognizes that human minds cannot
fully comprehend the mystery of Christ and the Spirit.*

THE UNIQUENESS AND UNIVERSALITY OF JESUS CHRIST (1974)

The Christian faith defines the purpose of existence to be love.
It proceeds from the singular happening in Jesus Christ and
acknowledges in Christ the definite meaning of reality in general. . . .

Therefore, the doctrine of the Trinity, which defines the divine
Persons as subsistent relations—as being *from* one another, *for*
one another, and *with* one another—is not a matter of abstract
speculation without any consequences for practical life. On the
contrary, it is the conscientious exegesis and exact representa-
tion of what in Jesus Christ is revealed to be the ultimate ground
and meaning of reality: Being as self-communicating love. Likewise, and for the same reason, the doctrine of the Trinity does
not represent a mythological or metaphysical objectification of
the Christian faith. It is rather, in its own way, a demythologi-
zation, i.e., de-objectification of the faith. It is the attempt to
think the Being of God in becoming [*Sein im Werden*], and thus,
according to its profoundest intention, a breakthrough to historical thought—without, of course, thereby betraying everything
to a groundless actualism or to a relativism that would render
everything a matter of indifference. It is ultimately not the case
that, as Kant would have it, the doctrine of the Trinity has absolutely nothing to offer in terms of praxis. On the contrary, this

is what gives the notion of "freedom determined by love" its profoundest justification.

For the believer, Jesus Christ is a sign that anticipates and really makes present the ultimate meaning of reality—a sign of hope. By definition hope is not something that can be substantiated (cf. Rom 8:24). Let us call it a hypothesis, which has to stand the test of time. Indeed, given the universality of its claim, such an experiment is [ultimately] coextensive with the experiment of life itself and the whole of [human] history. [As such], it can be decided with finality only at the end of time. In the meantime the believer can simply try to follow Jesus "in the Spirit," in the vicarious service of love for others, and thereby make of oneself a sign of this hope.   —EUU, 10–11

During his first year as the head of the Vatican's offices for Christian unity and religious relations with Jews, Kasper reiterated that the mystery of salvation manifests itself in the paradox of Christ's uniqueness and universality.

JESUS CHRIST, GOD'S DECISIVE WORD (2001)

If God has entirely, ultimately and unreservedly imparted God's self in the concrete person and history of Jesus Christ, then Jesus Christ is—to quote Anselm of Canterbury's *Proslogion*—"that than which nothing greater can be thought" ("*id quo maius cogitari nequit*"). Also, Jesus Christ is "that than which God can do nothing greater" ("*id quo Deus maius operari nequit*"). Seen in the light of the Christ-event, there cannot be any religion or culture which would surpass or supplement the Christian economy of salvation. Any truth or goodness found in other religions shares in what has been revealed in Jesus Christ in its fullness.

Nevertheless, no human being and also no dogma can ever entirely exhaust this mystery. According to the New Testament (Jn 16:13), God's Spirit is promised to us in order to lead us ever anew and ever deeper into the mystery. The encounter with other religions can be a way to open more deeply certain aspects of the one mystery of Christ. For this reason, interreligious dialogue is not a one-way street; it is an authentic encounter that can be enriching for us Christians. In this dialogue, we not only give but also learn and receive, because this is the key to understanding more fully the whole fullness of the mystery, given to us in Jesus Christ, in its entire length and breadth, height and depth (cf. Eph 3:18).

We are to work therefore in a Trinitarian and Christological framework in which to interpret unity and finality, a framework which is not totalitarian but which rather provides room [for other religions] and sets free. It is indeed part of the essence of true love that it unites on the most profound level without usurpation, thus leading the other to personal fulfillment.

These speculative and theoretical reflections take a concrete form when we look at the life of Jesus. As the gospels attest, Jesus is the human-for-others. He, the Lord, has come not to dominate but to serve and to give his life "for the many" (Mk 10:45 and parallels). He who emptied himself unto death is exalted and appointed the Lord of the cosmos (Phil 2:6–11). Thus self-consuming service is the new world order.

If the finality and universality of the Christian economy of salvation is understood in this way, then, on the one hand, it defines the Christian world mission as something essential to the church's nature and, on the other hand, it preserves and defends the freedom of each human being as well as the value and dignity of the various cultures. Precisely in its actual decisiveness, which opposes every form of syncretism and relativism, it grounds respectful, even dialogical and service-oriented relations with the other religions—relations that also reject every kind of fundamentalism with its narrow-mindedness. Understood in this way, the finality and universality of the Christian economy of salvation is no imperialistic claim which eviscerates or oppresses other religions. Even less does it justify and permit an imperialistic view of and an imperialistic approach to the church's mission. It has nothing to do with world domination, even though it has been occasionally misunderstood and misused in the church's history.

These dialogical and diachronic relations with other religions have three aspects. The confession of Jesus Christ as God's final and universal word affirms, respects and defends everything in other religions that is true, good, noble, and holy (cf. Phil 4:8); [this first aspect is] the *via positiva* or *via affirmativa*.

In a prophetic way, it criticizes whatever in the other religions is derogative to God's honor and the dignity of humans. This occurs by "mixing" divine and human elements so that neither God nor humans are respected in their proper dignity; [this second aspect is] the *via negativa* or *via critica et prophetica*.

Finally, it desires to invite other religions to attain their own fullness and realization by means of faith in Jesus Christ and participation in his fullness; [this third aspect is] the *via eminentiae*.

The Second Vatican Council's Decree on the Church's Missionary Activity (no. 9; cf. no. 11) integrates all three aspects by holding that everything that is good and true in the religions finds its norm in Jesus Christ and must be critically assessed in relation to Christ, purified and brought to fulfillment through him.

Understood in this way, the Christian confession—precisely because of its claim to finality and universality, which is objectionable to many people—is the call to and the foundation for mutual tolerance and respect, for sharing, communicating and exchanging, for understanding, reconciling and peace-making. It points to the One who is "the focal point of the desires of history and civilization," the One who is "the center of humanity, the joy of all hearts, and the fulfillment of all aspirations" (*Gaudium et Spes*, no. 45). —JCG, 18–26

Inspired and guided by the Second Vatican Council's and Pope John II's acknowledgment of God's irrevocable covenant with Jews and Judaism, Kasper energetically worked to clarify and advance Jewish–Christian relations.

JEWISH–CHRISTIAN RELATIONS TODAY (2007)

The Catholic Church exists—as the council affirmed—"in and out of local churches" which have their own responsibilities. Thus, in the aftermath of the council, many individual bishops' conferences established commissions for dialogue with Judaism and, in turn, issued important declarations. The collection of all these texts takes up two substantial volumes. . . .

In 2002, the International Council of Jews and Christians met in Montevideo, Uruguay; In July 2004, the meeting of the International Catholic–Jewish Liaison-Committee in Buenos Aires, Argentina, was without any doubt a highlight in our mutual relations and would not have been possible without strong support from the local level. . . .

I think it was a most significant step and a sign of the progress we made in Buenos Aires that we were able to embark on a practical social and charitable form of cooperation. Together, we successfully endeavored to help children who suffered the most in the tremendous economic crisis in Argentina. We hope that in the future, we can extend such activities in other parts of the world, too. The rabbinic tradition has expressed what is meant here in the sentence, "He who has saved one human being has saved the world." . . .

Jews and Christians together are a beacon of hope. For they can testify from the bitter and painful lessons of history that—despite otherness and foreignness and despite historical guilt—conversion, reconciliation, peace, and friendship are possible. May our century thus become a century of solidarity—shoulder to shoulder. Shalom!   —PTE, 8, 10–11

Kasper repeatedly upholds Vatican II's teaching that the Christian community along with the Jewish community "awaits the day, known to God alone, when all peoples will call on God with one voice and 'serve him shoulder to shoulder'" (Nostra Aetate, *no. 4).*

CHRISTIANITY AND JUDAISM TOWARD THE FUTURE (2007)

The proclamation that God is rich in mercy and hence opens a new future for humans is part of the oldest biblical traditions. It is therefore incorrect to juxtapose a supposedly vengeful God of the Old Testament with a New-Testament God of mercy, forgiveness and love. Jews and Christians share a common inheritance—and to a certain degree as well with Muslims, for each surah in the Quran begins with the acclamation of Allah's omnipotence and total mercifulness. In this aspect, the three monotheistic Abrahamic religions share a common heritage and, despite all undeniable differences, a common promise to a certain degree. It is important to emphasize this shared heritage in the interreligious dialogue; it is a foundational presupposition for world peace, because in the long run, peace cannot be guaranteed through military force but only through the deconstruction of prejudices and misunderstandings and the building of mutual understanding, respect, trust and, last but not least, justice. . . .

Christianity is a religion of the future (as is Judaism). It is not the religion of a static world but of a world of becoming, history, self-transcendence, future. Rahner would immediately add, though, that Christianity is the religion of the absolute future, which for him is just another way to say that the future of the human being is God and a life in God. This in turn means that Christianity does not postulate historical, programmatic, utopian ideologies. . . . The fact that Christianity is not a historical, immanent utopia does not mean, however, that the Christian hope would not matter to the historic, immanent future and therefore be historically irrelevant. . . . The hope for an *absolute* future reminds us that the history of the world is not the ultimate reality. . . . Historical success or failure, acknowledgment or disavowal do not determine the value of human beings or their actions. We do not have to—and cannot—build the reign of God or heaven on earth. Permanent peace and perfect happiness cannot exist in this temporal world. In this way, the history of this world becomes relativized, de-mythologized, de-ideologized and thereby humanized. The Christian hope for the future makes a person realistic and factual. . . . The ideology-critical aspect of Judeo–Christian hope becomes also evident in that it resists attempts to construct an inner, worldly ideology based on Christianity itself, hence remaining critical of forms of Integralism and fundamentalism which would like to construe scientific or political answers based on Scripture. It is as much impossible to derive a political manifesto from the Sermon on the Mount as it is to decide questions about evolution theory based on the creation account[s] in Genesis. . . .

This viewpoint must, of course, be complemented by a second aspect of hope that encourages historical action and accepts historical responsibility. . . . The rejection of Integralism and fundamentalism is the basis for a legitimate secularity but not for an ideological secularism that strives to expel religion and faith from the public sphere and to exile them into the sacristy. . . .

The absolute future as a future of truth, justice, love and life frees us from a nihilistic suspicion of futility that creeps up on us vis-à-vis historical incoherencies and continual natural catastrophes. It is therefore a critique of a fundamental relativism which claims that there is no authoritative order of values. It criticizes a paradigm in which the distinctions between truth and falsehood, justice and injustice, love and hatred or violence do not matter anymore and also in which decisions are rather based on egoistic pragmatism and ice-cold considerations of profit and personal gain.

In contrast to this attitude, the Judeo–Christian hope holds that it is never unreasonable and never irrational to do what is good, to take a stand for the truth, and to let justice prevail, to show mercy and to protect and save life. In the end, neither falsehood nor iniquity nor violence, neither money nor prestige nor domination will be the decisive factors. Rather, the future will belong to truth, justice, love and life. This way, the hope in an absolute future encourages and inspires us to take charge of our personal and communal historical future. A rabbinic proverb says: "Whoever saves *one* human being saves the world." . . .

If we take historical responsibility seriously, then the path into the historical future is not like a rocket which on its way into space simply ejects its burnt-out rocket-stages and leaves them behind. Rather, each change responsibly directed towards the future must neither ignore nature as the basis of our human existence, nor obliterate the positive inheritance of the past, much less recklessly and violently destroy it. . . .

Remembrance ought not either idealize or downplay the past. . . . On the contrary, remembrance should also recount history from the perspective of the victims, . . . of those who were left in the ditch, the neglected and the defeated. Remembrance must keep alive the unsettled possibilities of the past. In this way, remembrance becomes a dangerous memory which disrupts plausibilities, banalities and infatuations. It liberates from the ban of the present and thereby opens the future. This kind of remembrance is forward-moving remembrance; it is *memoria futuri*.

The new culture of remembrance resists ahistorical, lopsided scientific–technological thinking and the loss of historical consciousness. . . . Historical amnesia equates with identity loss and cultural decadence. It leads to relativistic whatever-ism and an addiction to the present and its moods. . . . It leads to the isolation of the individual and the atomization and disintegration of society. It renders one-sided progressivism confused and disoriented. . . .

The "memory of the passion of Christ," the *memoria passionis Christi*, is the center of the Christian liturgy. As the remembrance of Christ's death and resurrection, it is the remembrance of our own forgiveness and reconciliation. It opens the way for new evaluations of the dark and difficult aspects of our past and present in the light of this memory. It purifies our human memory and opens the possibility of cleansing bad memories that leave feelings of revenge, despair, hatred, resignation, bitterness, and frustration. It invites us to look anew at our unreconciled history with a reconciled heart, to forgive suffered injustice and to venture with former opponents into a new future.

We need such a culture of remembering that is simultaneously dangerous and reconciling. . . . The future is only possible for those who know their origins, cherish them and are able to make them fruitful for the future. The historically immanent future is not utopian. It is situated in the world and history; it is the future of the world and our history. . . .

I am personally convinced that the Jewish–Christian faith has not only a long history but also again a future. Perhaps we can recast the famous wager that Blaise Pascal presented: If you enter into religion's promise, you will lose absolutely nothing, but you may win everything, if nothing else, hope as the breath of life.   —ZVH, 97–104

Today, Cardinal Kasper is highly regarded around the world for his contributions to ecumenism and Jewish–Christian relations. Yet, as he recalls in his memoirs, he had no experiences throughout his early years in preparation for his leadership of the Pontifical Council for Promoting Ecumenism and also of the Commission for Religious Relations with the Jews.

THE CATHOLIC CHURCH'S TURN
TO ECUMENISM (2008)

As a boy, I would have never thought of entering a Protestant church. I would have thought that I should confess it. Dating a Protestant girl would have been a familial crisis, not only for our but also for her family. . . .

The shared experiences during the war brought Christians of both confessions closer to one another and laid the foundation for the process of rapprochement after the war. During that time, many churches had been destroyed, plus Protestant refugees [from the east] arrived in Catholic regions. . . . It was self-evident to open our churches to one another and to help out where we could. It was the beginning of a new togetherness among Christians. . . .

I knew Jews only from biblical narratives. In the village itself there were no signs of Jewish life, surely no synagogues. I remember only when during the catechesis, given by my mother, we talked about false teachings. I had asked her, "Where do the Nazis' teachings belong?" In response, she answered to the effect that the Nazis were fixated on race. What she meant by this, I did not understand at that time. I never heard expressions like "God murderers" either during religious classes in school or our catechesis at home. . . .

For me, Rome and the pope were far away. During the war, I knew of course that there was the pope and what he looked like. There was no television; the radio and newspapers were strictly censured. . . .

After 1945, Pius XII quickly attained high, indeed the highest esteem among Germans. The country was morally devastated, but the pope wanted to open for Germans the way back into the international community. Pius XII, who was the Vatican's nuncio to Germany from 1917 until 1929, appreciated the German culture and understood well that German culture and National Socialism were not the same and that not all Germans were National Socialists. —WHG, 23–24, 29

Cardinal Kasper's commitment to ecumenism arose in part because of his participation in the Catholic Tübingen School, which since its inception in 1817 has possessed an ecumenical orientation, especially evident in the work of Johann Adam Möhler.

Möhler is not only a name; it is also a program. Through his disputes with the enlightened theologians of his time as well as with the Father of modern Protestantism, Friedrich Schleiermacher, Johann Adam Möhler contributed to overcoming both controversial, theological polemics [between Catholicism and Protestants] and also dogmatic irenicism. Thus, he is rightly considered to be a forerunner and a pioneer of today's ecumenical theology, which proceeds no longer from what differentiates and separates but looks at the bigger common picture. In this way it views these differences in context, understands them better and then, when possible, overcomes them from our common heritage. . . .

Tübingen was shaped by Protestantism. Catholicism was lived on the margins. The Corpus Christi procession had to take place in the courtyard between St. John's Church and the Wilhelmstift seminary. It was unthinkable that Catholics would hold their procession through the city. Relationships between the Catholic and the Protestant faculties existed at best on a personal level but not institutionally. . . .

In the pre-conciliar period, a new way became evident. John XXIII's uncomplicated way of exercising the papal office opened the doors and windows of the church. The fact that something new was dawning was palpable, although it was not concretely formulated yet.

Despite or actually because of Pope Paul VI's efforts to do justice to as many factions as possible [at Vatican II], he became after the council one of the greatest reforming popes in the history of the church, taking courageous steps forward, not least in the area of ecumenism. His historic meeting with the Ecumenical Patriarch Athenagoras in Jerusalem on January 5 and 6, 1964, was the first of many, later meetings among high-ranking church officials—meetings that until then were unimaginable.

—WHG, 32, 34, 55

A milestone in ecumenism, according to Kasper, was Pope John Paul II's encyclical Ut Unum Sint *(1995), which was the first ecumenical encyclical in church history.*

Especially since my call to Rome [in 1999], Pope John Paul's stance toward ecumenism was important for me. At the beginning of his pontificate, not too many thought that this pope from Poland would achieve much, if anything. Yet, one was amazed at the ecumenical energy that he developed and at his accomplishments. His visits to other churches during his countless pastoral travels and his visit with the World Council of Churches in Geneva are unforgettable. . . .

To be sure, the ecumenical contacts have completely convinced me of one thing: the office of Peter is a gift of the Lord to his church. As one committed to ecumenism, one cannot do and pray enough that this gift is someday enlarged in a new, though essentially true form also in the other churches. . . .

Rome became an important center of ecumenism and a point of reference for many churches. Thus, despite the still existing separation, important elements of the unifying function of the Petrine office are now de facto implemented.

—WHG, 131–38

As Cardinal Kasper energetically undertook his work as the president of the Pontifical Council for Promoting Christian Unity and the chair of the Committee for Religious Relations with the Jews, he recognized that interpersonal relationships and the gift of the Holy Spirit are the wellspring for advances in ecumenism and Jewish–Christian relations.

With this [appointment] came countless trips throughout the world. They were exhausting but rewarding. One cannot engage in ecumenism just on paper or in scholarly dialogues. The ecumenical documents are certainly important, but they are paper. On Pentecost, the Holy Spirit came not in the form of academic publications but in the form of fire. The decisive elements in ecumenism, beside the fire of the Holy Spirit, are personal relationships, personal trust and personal friendships.

Thus, my life had radically changed once more. It had become interesting and exciting in a new way. It attained a new depth and breadth. I was allowed to see how I was participating, with my weak abilities, in the building of the church of the future and working toward the realization of the legacy that Jesus had bequeathed to us on the night before his suffering and death: "that they may be one" [Jn 17:11]. . . .

Only when each partner, through the eyes of faith, has recognized one's own faith, has true reconciliation happened. . . .

One cannot "make" this unity. One can neither cleverly organize it, nor attain it through diplomatic negotiations. Nor can one advanced it in sophisticated theological conversations. It is possible only as the gift of God's Spirit through a renewed Pentecost.   —WHG, 175, 190

Cardinal Kasper manifested great energy in promoting Jewish–Christian relations. Time and again, he has observed that Jewish faith and Christian faith are intimately connected.

ENGAGING IN JEWISH–CATHOLIC DIALOGUE (2008)

On the basis of the Old Testament, Judaism is essential to the foundations of Christianity, different from Hinduism or Buddhism, for example. It is not possible to define Christianity without the context of Judaism. To put it another way: Judaism and Christianity are not sister-churches but sister-religions. . . .

Already in 2001, I participated in the seventeenth meeting of the ILC [International Catholic Jewish Liaison Committee] in New York City. We saw each other again in 2004 in Buenos Aires and 2006 in Cape Town, South Africa. Moreover, in 2001, I traveled to the international congress of the International Council for Christians and Jews in Montevideo (Uruguay). . . .

When I was flying back from Montevideo in 2001, I had a similar experience to that of my first encounter with the Jewish delegation in Jerusalem. At my departure, a rabbi handed me a new Jewish prayer book. During the long flight, I began to read it and suddenly realized that, while reading, I was praying. It is true what a group of Jewish theologians formulated in their statement *Dabru emet* (September 2000) as a response to the Christian efforts for a new theology of Judaism: "Jews and Christians worship the same God." It is the God of Abraham, Isaac and Jacob who for us Christians is also the God of Jesus Christ.

Overall, the Jewish–Christian dialogue has advanced so well that the Chief Rabbi of Haifa, who is the Jewish co-moderator of the committee between the Holy See and Jerusalem's Great Rabbinate, could be invited to speak at the world synod of bishops in October 2008, giving a lecture on the Word of God in the tradition and practice of Judaism. This gesture meant more than thousands of words. . . .

Unfortunately, anti-Semitism is not just a phenomenon of the past; it has not disappeared at all. In this regard, one should not just think of the inflammatory diatribes of fundamentalist Islamic hotheads. We have to be vigilant, too, first and foremost in eastern parts of Europe. For this reason, we chose the theme "Religion and Civil Society Today" for the meeting of the unity committee in November 2008 in Budapest. . . .

In the face of the political conflicts in the Near East, a Jewish–Christian dialogue with Islam bears a challenge. We believed that we should accept it and started a so-called trialog jointly with the Council for Interreligious Dialogue in collaboration with the institute *Tres culturas* in Seville. . . .

—WHG, 280, 279, 282, 286, 283, 287

In his discussions of the relationship between Christianity and Judaism, Kasper often observes that Christians and Jews will have their respective views far surpassed at the coming of God's messianic age and the Messiah. In this regard, he appeals to Zechariah 14:9 and Zephaniah (Sophoniah) 3:9 as well as to Vatican II's Declaration on the Relation of the Church to Non-Christian Religions, Nostra Aetate, no. 4.

In the book of the prophet Zechariah there is a beautiful image for the relationship of Jews and Christians, to which *Nostra Aetate* also refers: when the Messiah comes, we will stand shoulder to shoulder. Not confronting each other, but—albeit distinct—shoulder to shoulder, in solidarity in our common service for the peace and salvation of the world. . . .

—WHG, 296

In his memoir, Cardinal Kasper conveys his vision of the Christian faith in the twenty-first century.

CATHOLICISM AND THE WORLD RELIGIONS (2008)

What is labelled today as globalization is actually nothing new. Christianity was always global in its origins and missions. It is, so to speak, the oldest global player. "Go, therefore, and make disciples of all nations" is the charge of Jesus [Mt 28:19]. From the beginning, world mission was inextricably linked with dialog. One thinks of the speech of the apostle Paul at the Areopagus in Athens: "What therefore you unknowingly worship, I proclaim to you" [Acts 17:23]. No one would seriously maintain that Paul would have forgotten in the process the distinct Christian [identity] and this call to mission. Mission, rightly understood, is a dialogical endeavor.

I predict that, at the beginning of the third millennium, Christianity stands on the threshold of a new epoch in its history. In the first millennium, Christianity spread throughout Europe. In the second millennium, it spread into the Americas and Africa. The third millennium could be the millennium of Asia.

Considering the relations to newly emerging world powers such as China and India, this constitutes not only a political challenge. It also involves the encounter with Asia's religions and cultures which, in the past, have not been compatible with Christianity.   —WHG, 298

*Cardinal Kasper has remained active in Jewish–Christian dia-
logue, even though he stepped aside in 2010 as the head of the
Commission for Religious Relations with the Jews.*

THE FUTURE OF JEWISH–
CHRISTIAN DIALOGUE (2011)

The common heritage of Jews and Christians includes the joint
vocation to a common witness to the one God and his commandments. This includes the unmasking and prophetic criticism of the new false-gods and idols of our time, and a shared
commitment to human dignity, to justice and peace in the world,
to the dignity and worth of the family, and to the integrity of creation. Not least, Jews and Christians can give witness together
to the dialogue, cooperation and reconciliation that are possible
even after a difficult and complex history. Likewise, they can
stand together for *teshuvah*, i.e., for repentance and reconciliation. Moreover, with the celebration of the Sabbath or Sunday,
they perform an indispensable service for the freedom of people:
they are showing that in this world there should be a sacred time
dedicated to God and that being human should not be reduced
to labor, economics, business, and pleasure.

Above all, Jews and Christians look to the future: they give
witness together—in the midst of the many dilemmas and
instances of hopelessness in the world—to the hope for perfect
justice and the universal *shalom* that God alone will usher in
at the end of time. Thus, they contribute to building a just and
humanitarian world in which such a terrible event as the Shoah
cannot be repeated. That the dialogue in the not-too-distant
future may also help to promote a peace process in the Middle
East is, unfortunately, thus far an unrealized wish of all parties.

No one could have foreseen forty-five years ago where we are
today in the relationship between Jews and Christians. We have
advanced farther than we could have imagined back then. But
today we also see more clearly that the road to each other and

with each other is not complete and still has a long way to go. *Nostra Aetate* is far from being a finished agenda.

—FCJ, xvii–xviii

Kasper continues to work for ecumenism, although he is no longer the president of the Pontifical Commission for Promoting Christian Unity. Confident in the Holy Spirit's presence, Kasper faces the future with hope.

THE FUTURE OF ECUMENISM (2012)

In the last fifty years, we have accomplished much, much more than many had anticipated fifty years ago. However, there still lies in front of us a difficult stretch which most probably will be longer than many others had hoped at that time. Current indications are that we are reaching the end not of the ecumenical movement itself but of the form which the ecumenical movement has taken during the twentieth century and which has borne much good fruit and that, in the still young twenty-first century, we must find new ways and new forms in order to remain true to Jesus' charge to be one and to give joint witness. We ought not and may not abort the dialogues, even when they become tiresome. In the new phase, we rather ought gratefully to take up, pursue and deepen everything that was given to us in the past century. A phase of the ecumenical movement is coming to an end, not the ecumenical movement itself.

In this new phase, all churches, especially those in our western, secularized world, are going through difficult, inner crises of faith. It is most important therefore to secure the common bases of faith, to keep them alive and vibrant: the faith in the one God, in the one Lord Jesus Christ, in the working of the Holy Spirit in the church through word and sacrament and common hope in eternal life. Without this common foundation, all ecumenical efforts are suspended between the sky and the earth; without a common basis of faith our joint witness in the world becomes pointless.

These common, basic Christian truths must be newly appropriated by every generation. In the past epoch, which was largely shaped by Christianity, this process could be more or less presupposed. For today's emerging younger generation, being a Christian is no longer self-evident. They are not so much concerned with the ecumenical process but with the foundational decision for a Christian life and their specific identity as a Catholic, Protestant or Orthodox Christians. Therefore, today the introduction to the common, basic Christian truths must have priority.

Moreover, in today's world that widely lacks an orientation, most of the confessional distinctions have moved from the dogmatic level to questions related to way-of-life and ethics. These questions include the protection of human life from conception to natural death, a human being's God-given dignity and the fundamental human rights, marriage and the family, the responsible consideration of human sexuality and the difficult new questions in the field of bio-ethics. In these areas, the dialogue between churches is unfortunately more difficult in our world but also more urgent. Hence, we have to put forth an effort to find common answers to these questions, based on the shared foundation of the Ten Commandments and the ethical directions found in the gospels. Only in this way can we together be the salt of the earth and light of the world.

As institutional ecumenism has entered a difficult phase in regards to these issues, in which quick progress can hardly be expected, there is forming a liberal Catholic–Protestant ecumenism which ignores the differences and is going its own way. I have great doubts about whether this kind of ecumenism can have a future, or whether it will come sooner or later to an end. In the meantime, there is quietly emerging a second, more spiritual ecumenism which is returning to the sources of ecumenism. In this, various ecumenical groups of Catholic, Orthodox and Protestant Christians, often from spiritual communities and movements, who are faithful to the Bible and the Christian confessions of faith, are meeting regularly for the reading of and the reflecting on sacred scripture, for spiritual conversations and prayer as well as for ongoing theological education, and in gratitude they discover how close they actually are to one another. To use computer words, these spiritual cells are building through their interconnections a growing worldwide, invisible cloister, as Paul Couturier envisioned. Most of all, I bank on great hope for this spiritual ecumenism.   —VEW, 30–33

7

Christian Hope

The Word of God, through whom all things were made, was made flesh, so that as a perfect man he could save all women and men and sum up all things in himself. The Lord is the goal of human history, the focal point of the desires of history and civilization, the center of humanity, the joy of all hearts, and the fulfillment of all aspirations. It is he whom the Father raised from the dead, exalted and placed at his right hand, constituting him judge of the living and the dead. Animated and drawn together in his Spirit we press onwards on our journey towards the consummation of history which fully corresponds to the plan of his love: "to unite all things in him, things in heaven and things on earth" (Eph 1:10).

—Gaudium et Spes, no. 45

In 1965, the Second Vatican Council conveyed its Christian vision of creation and history in its Pastoral Constitution on the Church, Gaudium et Spes. *Seven years later, Walter Kasper elaborated on this vision in his book* An Introduction to the Christian Faith, *which includes reflections on a Christian sense of humor and joy. In this book and later writings, Kasper often observes that authentic Christian faith nurtures joy and hope, and hence "joyful hope." In other words, he reiterates* Gaudium et Spes, no. 45: "Lord is the goal of human history, . . . the joy of all hearts, and the fulfillment of all aspirations."

CHRISTIAN JOY (1972)

In the person of Jesus Christ, a fundamentally new way of understanding human existence manifests itself. . . . Self-communicating and radiating love is placed first in Christianity. Love is the very definition of God (1 Jn 4:8). God's sovereign freedom in love shows itself in the fact that it pours itself unrestrictedly—even unto death and beyond it—to humans, without losing itself in this outpouring. Impotence becomes the expression of power; foolishness, the wisdom of God (cf. 1 Cor 1:17–31).

If we want to talk about the revolutionary power of Christian faith, then here is the place because this revolution shakes the foundations of life. Whoever tries to construe out of this a revolutionary, political program has not understood the essence of this kind of trans-valuation of all values, nor has anyone who attempts to employ Christianity as an ideology to undergird the status quo. Both are legalism.

The Christian faith is not characterized by a rigid legal system nor by an individual or common program but by exuberance, abundance and insouciance. This must indeed be perceived as foolishness in a society whose standards are performance and efficiency. But precisely this foolishness loosens the shackles of the inhumane compulsion to prove oneself—and [to test] others—through ever rising levels of performance. Without becoming a quietist, it opens the door into a reconciled, joyful and truly human existence. Christian faith results in joy. According to the New Testament, joy is one of the anticipatory signs of the eschatological reality.

Therefore, a sense of humor is the foremost characteristic of the Christian faith. The lack of a sense of humor and the huffiness which have widely spread throughout today's church and theology are probably one of the gravest accusations against the current state of Christianity. A sense of humor is distinct, of

course, from the enraptured or almost tart smile of some pathet-
ically "cheerful saints." Humor is an attitude that allows humans
to be fully human and merely human because it permits only
God to be God and thereby exposes the laughableness of all
other claims for absolute grandeur and recognition. God "who
sits in heaven laughs" (Ps 2:4). Hence, the correct distinction
between God and humans is the opposite of the deadly seri-
ousness of sin. It is the reason for salvation, and it allows us to
be joyful. This joy is one of the foundational expressions of the
Christian faith.   —EIG, 120–21

*In "The Issue of Evil" (see Chapter 1), Walter Kasper
acknowledges the influence of evil on human affairs, the inability of contemporary society to name evil as evil, and the validity
of the church's language in relation to evil. As he explains below,
Christian belief views evil within the horizon of God's salvific
presence and action in history and hence speaks of evil in negative terms, as expressed in the renunciations declared at baptism.
The Spirit will bring humankind in Christ beyond all forms of
evil. As stated in* Gaudium et Spes, *no. 45: "Animated and drawn
together in the Spirit we press onwards on our journey towards
the consummation of history which fully corresponds to the
plan of his love."*

EVIL AND ESCHATOLOGY (1978)

Biblical Testimony

The biblical testimony gives a multifaceted answer to the question of the origin of evil. It speaks of the personal sins of humans,
of a governing power of sin above the human community, and of
evil "powers and principalities." While this multifaceted answer
ultimately forms a whole, it cannot be reduced to one facet
among the many facets. . . .

According to scripture, neither angels nor demons, i.e., the
devil, derogate from the intimacy between humans and God,

nor from humans' personal responsibility before God and hence
from their freedom. Creation has its fulfillment in the economy
of salvation. This fulfillment, though, consists in the history of
God and humans that reaches its culmination in Jesus Christ.
In this history of God with humans, angels serve only as God's
messengers. Through them, the entirety of reality is drawn into
the economy of salvation. The same is true for evil forces. They
express the universal–cosmic dimension of the need for redemption and of redemption itself. In history, only humans can initiate misery by refusing God's offer [of salvation]. Still humans
concretely bring about evil in a concrete way when they relinquish themselves to an active power of evil instead of respecting
God and God's order.

Angels and demons have roles not at the center of the Gospel but clearly at its margins. They present its furthermost cosmic horizon and, in this, they give to biblical belief in salvation
its universal–cosmic perspective, a perspective which is rather
more an unarticulated horizon than a formulated content. They
are literally marginal truths. . . . The Bible's talk about angels
and the devil, i.e., demons, is symbolic discourse concerning
the world's eschatological meaning, specifically the universal–
cosmic meaning of the redemptive act of Jesus Christ.

The Reality and Un-Reality of Evil

The relative importance and pertinence of biblical testimony
concerning the "powers and principalities" opposing God and
humans lead to the quest for a more precise essential determination of evil. Based on our review so far, we can approach this
topic only with exceptional caution and circumspection. . . . In
this regard, symbol and reality do not stand in opposition to
each other. Rather, by definition, symbols disclose reality. In the
end, human reason experiences evil as an impenetrable mystery.
Not without reason, scripture speaks therefore of the *mysterium
iniquitatis* ["mystery of iniquity"]. . . .

We must start our reflection at the center of the biblical testimony: God's universal, eschatological saving act in Jesus Christ is the final evidence for the vacuity of the evil powers and principalities. Scripture calls demons "nothings," thereby actually achieving the essential determination of evil. In the following, we try to interpret the reality of evil accordingly as that which is negation, nothingness, before God. . . .

From a theological perspective, evil cannot be purely ontologically defined as a lack of good but only in relation to God, as a deficiency before God, as the inversion of the relation to God. Evil is that created entity, endowed with freedom, which does not acknowledge the significance of its created existence and wants to be like God. Searching for the meaning of its existence in opposition to God, it can find this meaning only in vacuity and must therefore become vacuous. This means that vacuity is different from nothingness. Evil is vacuity, but it is not nothing. . . .

One cannot help but characterize the evil powers and principalities as personally structured beings with an intelligence and a will [albeit] only in a very analogous way. The devil does not have a personified form but a non-form, self-annihilating into anonymity and facelessness, a being which perverts itself into a non-being, a person in the form of a non-person. . . . We cannot and ought not create therefore a concrete image of the devil, as it is in a mode of disintegration and annihilation of itself. It is the self-perpetuating self-destruction and, at the same time, the destruction of all cosmic order. Although the devil can loosen and untether those possibilities excluded in the reality of creation, it cannot master them. They will become too much so that the devil will stand like the Sorcerer's Apprentice who cannot ban the spirits that were called forth. It is damned by its own deed.

Hence, the mystery of evil leads not to one specific definition. In the last analysis, it is not about ontological speculation but about soteriology. It generates . . . talk about the center of Christian faith: the message of the new creation in Jesus Christ, through which God has re-established the divinely intended peace and reconciliation not only in humans but also in the whole cosmos. In this new beginning, the evil powers and principalities have proven once and for all to be vacuous; they are to be held up for mockery and disgrace. . . .

Christian Life

The Christian faith and above all the question of evil are not only a theoretical issue but also a pressing practical matter. . . .

First, talk about evil is possible only indirectly. Since evil is absurdity, contradiction and irrationality, it cannot be presented in a systematic order. Because the devil is the parasite per se, it can be spoken of only as a sort of negating of the message of salvation through God's eschatological victory, at the margin in relation to the salvation of the world . . . Therefore, in the theological sense of the word, someone cannot believe in the devil. The act of belief is oriented solely to God, to Jesus Christ and the Holy Spirit. . . . Someone cannot believe in the devil; one can only reject it. The language used in the baptismal ceremony, drawing on the ancient tradition, has great significance. It expresses that we can speak of the devil only in the form of an emphatic rejection. We can encounter the power of the negative only through the negation of the negation and this means from the firm point of faith. Without this negation, our stance would not be authentic. Therefore, the negative form of talk about the devil is inseparably linked to the baptismal ceremony . . . [and] it cannot be separated from the Christian and ecclesial confession of faith.

Second, the once-and-for-all rejection of the power of evil at baptism must become in the life of the baptized Christian [an awareness of] being constantly alert to evil. Christians should not be the least naïve and clueless; they must know about the reality of evil and reckon to encounter it. . . . The traditional rules concerning the discernment of spirits aim in this direction [cf. Gal 5:19–23]. As signs of the activity of God, there count among others: love, peace, joy, interior peace and serenity, patience, sincerity, openness, and especially acknowledgement of the truth. . . .

Third, most important in the pastoral and spiritual engagement with the issue of evil is the prayer, "deliver us from the evil one" [Mt 6:13]. Theological discourse about evil directs us to preserve and encourage this prayer. It expresses both unconditional trust in the power of God and also our taking serious the powers of evil. In this prayer, the power of evil is concretely overcome. In it, humans create space for God and God's reign. In it, the initial, intention of creation comes to realization. It frames the reality of evil in the only appropriate way, that is, in relation to the hope for the definite revelation of the reign of God in which finally all diabolic confusion and all deception in the world will finally end.

With this "ordinary" and daily prayer of all Christians concerning deliverance from evil as the background, we can appreciate anew and in greater depth exorcism which is the ritualized, official prayer in the name of Christ and the church for deliverance from the power of the devil. An exorcism presupposes the efforts of physicians. Even in the case of a "normal" illness, Christians who are appropriately informed about their faith hold that going to a physician and simultaneously praying for health are not mutually exclusive. Vice-versa, prayer for someone who is suffering does not remove the obligation to seek medical assistance to the extent that it is humanly possible. Moreover, exorcism was never intended to isolate and stigmatize. The solemn official prayer of the church is rather meant to express in its true interior meaning the solidarity of all members of the church with a suffering individual. . . . The official prayer of deliverance from the power of evil, understood properly and responsibly practiced, is rather intended to bestow or restore that freedom for which Jesus Christ has freed us. A correctly understood theology of exorcism leads therefore to a critique of many current practices of exorcism and thus to the demand for their revision.

In general, the misuse of something should not stop the appropriate use of it. In the case of exorcism, it demands the appropriate use all the more. The solemn and official prayer of the church for deliverance from the power of evil actually prevents experiences of reality—which arise repeatedly, contrary to all simple ideologies from the Enlightenment—either from being relegated to the unmonitored domain of sub-cultures and thereby eventually being suppressed, or from being the cause for the isolation of the individual in an apathetic culture of analgesics (L. Kolakowski), the individual who is then left alone with pain and problems.

For this reason, theology cannot depart from the symbols, categories and formulations in the Christian tradition which interpret evil. Rather, it must discuss these in dialogue with the modern sciences and thus break open their reality and remind us of their hope-giving potential. Theology must take care therefore that this hope-giving, liberating potential not be lost or reversed into the opposite. Precisely in regard to the question of evil, service to the human community demands from theologians a service to tradition.   —TPB, 60–69

Christian hope is a theme that Walter Kasper has woven throughout his writings. As he observes, it is a fruit of the church's belief in Jesus Christ as savior and in the Holy Spirit's saving presence and action in human affairs.

LIVING WITH HOPE (1985)

The last sentence of the [Nicene] Creed—"We look forward to the resurrection of the dead and the life of the world to come"— is the Christian answer to the primordial hope of humans. This answer is somewhat near to us contemporary people, and yet it is at the same time deeply alien to many. It is near to us as a *prospect of hope*. For hope is profoundly human. No human being can live without hope. Hope is different from simple optimism, which expects things to work out somehow. Hope, however, reaches deeper and wider. It is the future-oriented expectation that the drab routine and the burdens of daily living, the inequality and injustice in the world, and the reality of evil and suffering will not have the final word and are not the ultimate reality. Hope holds therefore that reality is open. This expectation obviously remains ambiguous. Especially today there exists anxiety among people before the threats of the future. The strongest objection to all purely interior hope is death. Basically, humans have never come to terms with the inevitability of death. Thus, all religions in some way speak about hope which transcends death. The question "What may we hope for?" is not just a religious question; it is also one of the primordial human questions. It is inseparable from the question: what remains, what holds up, what is the meaning of life, of the world, of history? What is our purpose in life on earth? . . . .

Facing such questions, the Christian faith is challenged today in special ways to give a justification of the hope which fills us (1 Pet 3:15). In order to give this, we must first of all be sure of the foundation of Christian hope. The starting point, the *basis of Christian hope*, is not some kind of wishful thinking, projection and speculation; it is no cheap optimism in a fortunate outcome, no "Principle of Hope" [Ernst Bloch], and no belief in progress, in evolution or revolution. In faith, we are only able to say something about our future because this future has already begun in Jesus Christ. It is the fundamental conviction, indeed the core of Christian faith that Jesus Christ is the first of those raised from the dead (Rom 8:29; 1 Cor 15:20; Col 1:18). *The basis and continuing measure of our hope is therefore the resurrection of Jesus Christ.* Everything that we as Christians can say about our resurrection to eternal life is only the unfolding and the extrapolating of the fundamental confession of faith concerning Jesus

Christ, his resurrection and his exaltation. Precisely because we are united through faith and baptism with Jesus Christ and his death, we may also hope to be united with his resurrection (Rom 6:5). St. Augustine articulated well this link [between faith and resurrection]: "Christ has accomplished what is still hope for us. What we hope for, we do not see. However, we are the body of that head in which there is already the reality that we await."

According to sacred scripture, it is the *work of the Holy Spirit* to take up all of creation into the new creation and transfiguration that has begun in Jesus Christ. This is the reason why the statements concerning our faith in the life of the world to come conclude the third part of the Creed, which in its entirety is devoted to the work of the Holy Spirit.

—KAT, 398–400

As Kasper explains, the Second Vatican II Council attests in Gaudium et Spes *that the basis of Christian hope is Jesus Christ.*

HOPE IN JESUS CHRIST (1985)

The confession of faith concerning the coming of Jesus Christ in glory at the end of time as judge of the living and the dead has imprinted itself deep within the Christian consciousness. We need only to think the gospels on the coming of Christ on the clouds of heaven [e.g., Mk 13:26] which, according to the lectionary of the old and new liturgy, are read every year on the last Sunday of the church year and also on the first Sunday of Advent. No one can hear them without sensing a deep interior shaking. We also can consider the classic paintings of the Last Judgment or the prayers and songs expressing hope and fear, beginning with fervent, hope-filled early Christian call, "Maranatha!," "Our Lord, come!" (1 Cor 16:22) and up to the very different "*Dies irae*" ["Day of wrath"] in the old Requiem, the Mass for the dead. Thus, the article of faith "from there he will come to judge the living and the dead" [Apostles' Creed], is both based in biblical testimony itself and also deeply rooted in the faith and prayer of the church, indeed in its entire life. In doctrinal theology, this article constitutes part of the teaching about the "Last Things": the resurrection of the dead, the Last Judgment with eternal redemption or condemnation, the new heaven, and the new earth. . . .

The message of the final coming of Jesus Christ in glory is not a theory (in the modern sense of the term), nor of course merely a visceral impulse, but simultaneously a consolation and a claim. An emphasis on the divine mystery of the precise day and hour follows the admonition: "Be watchful! Be alert!" (Mk 13:33).

The consolation contained in the article of faith concerning the final coming of Jesus Christ in glory conveys hope in the final victory of life and love over the powers of death and violence, the victory of truth and justice over the world's bewildering swirl of lies and injustice in the world that cry out to heaven. This certitude of hope in God's final Yes and Amen to creation and to humans (2 Cor 1:20) necessarily includes the idea of judgment. For how could there be a final judgment without a final separation of good from evil! Only in this way can hope seriously hold that love never gives out but always remains (1 Cor 13:8). It conveys: "Love and its works remain" (*Gaudium et Spes*, no. 39). Since God's love through Jesus Christ in the Holy Spirit is *the* eschatological reality, everything which is done in love and out of love will ultimately remain; it is permanently established in reality.

In this light, the hope in the new heaven and the new earth is anything else but an empty promise. It does not remove our responsibility for this earth but obliges and encourages us to work for a civilization of love (Pope Paul VI). It engages our imagination and our initiative; it criticizes all conformity to and toleration of the existing state of affairs. To be sure, we cannot build the reign of God, but in love we can and ought to "give a constructive sketch of the world to come" (General Synod of the West-German Bishops, 1975). To be sure, the fragmentary anticipation of the future glory is possible only through the death of

Christ and through our dying with Christ. The patient enduring of suffering and persecution is therefore the preparatory epiphany of the future glory (2 Cor 4:7 ff.). As we know, patience is neither weakness nor resignation; it is, so to speak, the long breath of hope in the final coming of Jesus Christ and the passion for the coming reign of God. It knows that "these are not mixed together in eternity"; "*Non confundar in aeternum*" ["Let me not be put to shame in eternity"; see Ps 31:2; *Te Deum*].

—HJC, 13–14

Beginning with the Second Vatican Council, the Catholic Church has sought to retrieve its eschatological orientation as expressed in Gaudium et Spes, *no. 45: "we press onwards on our journey towards the consummation of history." Kasper has contributed to this renewed attentiveness to the coming of God's "Last Age." Once again, he stresses the theological virtue of hope.*

INDIVIDUAL SALVATION AND ESCHATOLOGICAL CONSUMMATION (1994)

Hope is not a commodity that people either have or do not have; hope is of the very essence of human existence. When there is no hope for the future, life becomes completely meaningless. The question of the future is thus both the focus and the paradigm of the question of human salvation.

The current situation presents a particular challenge to Christians. They are required to bear public witness to the hope that is in them (cf. 1 Pet 3:15). In the face of the questions, fears, conflicts and hopes of the world in which we live, they must ensure that they are a living witness to the potential for hope that is central to Christian belief. . . .

The crucial question which emerged was whether and to what extent the Greek metaphysical view of the personal immortality of the soul was compatible with the biblical expectation of a general resurrection of the body at the end of time. Or, to put it another way: What is the relationship between personal eschatology where the individual is judged after death, and universal eschatology, which involves the second coming of Christ to judge the world? . . .

One important point of access to the problem at hand is provided by a passage from Origen's seventh homily on the book of Leviticus. Origen says: "You will enter into joy then if you leave this life in holiness. But your full joy will only come when not one of your members is lacking. Wherefore you must wait for others, just as others have waited for you. Surely, too, if you who are a member have not perfect joy as long as a member is missing, how much more will he, our Lord and Savior, consider his joy incomplete while any member of his body is missing. . . . He is loath to receive his perfect happiness without you, that is, without his people who constitute his body and his members" (quoted in Henri de Lubac, *Catholicism* [1964], p. 239).

This text shows that salvation and judgment concern individual persons. However, the individual is and has its being in relation to others. This means that the individual cannot reach a perfected state until all other human beings have reached that state as well. Individual and general eschatology are therefore essentially interdependent. This train of thought is also fully compatible with the biblical conception of the body. In the Bible, the term body does not just mean corporeality, but rather embraces each and every aspect of being human. Nor does the Bible see a human being as a hermetically closed personality. Instead, the individual is woven into the whole fabric and history of the world, including its solidarity and intercommunication. Correspondingly, death, according to the Old Testament, is synonymous with entry into "Sheol." Yet, the essence of Sheol is lack of communication. Seen from this perspective, the resurrection of the dead is a process in which the full communication which has been interrupted by death is restored and in which everything finds its place.

Yet, human beings love not only in relation to other human beings but also in relation to their environment. Having a body, they are part of the environment. Conversely, through the body, the world is part of the human being. One can even say that the material world acquires meaning only in the corporeality of human beings. This anthropocentric worldview has foundations in the apocalyptic thinking of the Bible. Through the first Adam's decision to be disobedient, the whole cosmos is subjected to being in a transitory condition. Through the obedience of the new Adam, through his death and his exaltation, the whole cosmos is redeemed (Cf. Gn 1–3; Rom 5:12–21; 1 Cor 15:21–23, 45–49). Thus, the individual and indeed humanity as a whole cannot reach their consummate form until the whole cosmos has been brought to consummation as well.

But cosmic consummation is more than just the ripe fruit of evolution and history. It is more than the successive harvesting or absorption of time into the dimension of eternity. It must rather be viewed as something new, as a new creative act of God. For only the Creator has unlimited access to and control over natural and cosmic conditions. But there is also another important reason why cosmic consummation must be regarded as a creative act of God. History does not simply mature into a state of perfection; history is rather the scene of the battle that is constantly raging between the kingdom of God and its opponent, the kingdom of evil. Theodicy and anthropodicy require that the conflict between truth and falsehood, justice and injustice be resolved and that absolute justice be established. In a word: there must be an end to all nonsense. It is the fulfillment of this very basic hope that is meant when scripture talks in apocalyptic language about the Lord in the end destroying his adversary, who refuses to acknowledge God's holiness and shows nothing but contempt for human dignity.

The details of how the consummation of the world and of history are to be achieved through the fire of the last judgment remain a mystery to which only God knows the answer. Since God is and remains a mystery, there is no place for foreknowledge or calculations in this matter. Nor can there be any concrete depictions of the final state. All that hope requires is the certitude that the eschatological event is a reality, the knowledge that God is faithful and that God has accepted the world definitively in Jesus Christ. The world and its history are therefore not at the mercy of arbitrary forces. Instead, at the end of time, God will be "all in all" (1 Cor 15:28). Every believer can therefore say with conviction: "*Non confundar in aeternum*" ["Let me never be put to shame in eternity" (see Ps 31:2; *Te Deum*)].

—ISE, 8–9, 12, 16–18

At an early age, Cardinal Kasper became aware of the fleeting character of human life. During the first thirteen years of his life, he saw the lives of his family and neighbors disrupted and often destroyed by Nazism and the Second World War. These experiences of loss likely influenced Kasper's reflections on the Nicene Creed's final sentence: "We look forward to the resurrection of the dead and the life of the world to come."

EXPERIENCES OF LOSS (2008)

During wartime, one learned geography in a downright perverse manner by listening to the reports of front-movements and battles that mentioned cities, rivers and regions and also to relatives and friends who fought in Russia or in the Crimea. An uncle and a cousin, who was just a few years older than I, were there and never returned. Also, the fiancé of an older cousin neither. She remained unmarried, staying true to him until the end of her life. . . .

When public transportation no longer worked, I had to switch over to my bicycle. According to today's standards, it was a quite old bone-shaker, without gears by that time; again and again, it had flat tires which I myself repaired. When enemy fighter bombers dived, one had to take shelter in the ditches, dug out along the sides of the road. . . . Some relatives whose houses were destroyed moved to Wäschenbeuren. We had to make space for each other. . . . Still today I hear the screaming of the children during the ear-deafening machine-gun fire of the fighter bombers. Our house too was damaged, one side was riddled by shellfire. Then came the parents searching for their children. When the French troops finally moved in, there were also German soldiers with us in a basement. As the French soldiers came down one set of stairs, the German soldiers fled up the other staircase into the open, and we as civilians were in the middle. The French soldiers held each one of us at gunpoint . . . . That was really awful. . . .

—WHG, 16–18

Kasper has also experienced loss during his adult years and sought consolation in the promise of eternal life in Jesus Christ.

In all of these eventful years, important to me was the friendship with my colleague in the seminary and ordination Josef Schupp, who also grew up in the Allgäu. . . . Many Sunday afternoons, we walked together for hours through the nearby Schönbuch. Also, we hiked together through the Allgäu during vacations; we conversed with one another and affirmed each other. . . . Unfortunately, he died quite suddenly during the *sede vacante* after the death of Rottenburg's Bishop Moser. At the time, he was handling alone the [diocesan] personnel problems that had enmeshed him and had "broken" him within. His death left a void for me. . . .

An even bigger loss were the deaths of my parents. They liked to come to Tübingen each Easter and shared in what was going on in my life. My mother passed away after a long illness in December 1981, and my father followed her just six years later, March 1987. I was blessed to celebrate the funeral liturgy for both of them in Wangen. Their lives were filled with work and fully dedicated to family and children. In the forest cemetery of St. Wolfgang, they found their last rest in God's eternity.

It is a common experience, I think. The death of one's parents is a bitter break in one's life. In a certain sense, only then does one fully enter into adulthood and also becomes lonelier. Fortunately, we as a family have remained close to each other— my sisters and my brother-in-law. The family home in Wangen became our common point of reference where we meet on a regular basis. —WHG, 85–86

LOOKING AHEAD (2008)

On his seventy-fifth birthday, Kasper presided at a Mass with his family and friends at the tomb of St. Peter. He concluded his homily with these words:

Looking to the future, there is not much remaining after seventy-five years. The one certainty is that one has most of his years behind him. We must place what remains in the hands of the Other and hope that God deals graciously with us.

In this regard, the Gospel of John speaks a beautiful and consoling word: "Remain in my love, . . . so that my joy may be in you and your joy may be complete" (Jn 15:9b, 11). "Remain" is a fundamental word in the Fourth Gospel. It is a consoling word, for it assures us that in this uncertain, quickly changing world, we have what remains, a home which no one can take from us; what remains exists in God's love, and already in this world we are raised up to what remains. Further, what remains is the eternal reality in which our joy will be complete. As Christians, we know that at the end our life is not lost, that it does not seep into a brooklet in the desert of nothingness, but that it will flow into the infinite ocean of complete joy.

When and how that will be, we do not know; and this is good. During these days, everyone is wishing me that this may not happen soon, for eternity is indeed long. At this Eucharist,

I'd like to put into the chalice everything that has occurred in our lives until now, and—as it now says in the liturgy—ask that God may accept our sacrifice to be in praise of God and for the salvation of the entire world, that God may purify this sacrifice and transform it, that God may make it fruitful for many other people and for the entire holy church.   —WHG, 317

Continuing his reflection on "Sacred Signs" (see Chapter 1), Kasper explains that the future is already breaking into the present, that a foretaste of the feast in the eschaton is available today in the church's worship and sacraments. In order to make the sacred more readily accessible in our secular society, the church needs to undertake a radical renewal of its "liturgical-sacramental culture."

SACRAMENTAL SIGNS (2012)

Let us talk about sacred signs. In the Old Testament, things related to cult have religious significance: the Ark, the sacred ointments and more. In the New Testament, this meaning is surpassed by a symbolic interpretation, foreshadowing the New Covenant. But this [change] does not mean that the New Testament does not know sacred signs any more.

Bread and wine are understood—in later terminology—as sacramental signs, likewise, water at baptism, the oil for anointing, and the laying on of hands at ordination. Paul insists on the distinctions among the sacramental breaking of the bread, a shared dinner, and a fraternal agape (1 Cor 11:29) . . . This [insistence] shows that not everything is the same; that we have to distinguish between a sacramental and a profane meal, between the sacramental and the profane table, between the Eucharist and an agape celebration.

This leads us back to the question if some liturgical celebrations really maintain the distinctiveness of the sacred and the reverence before the Holy. [It seems that] we have to re-learn the awe and therefore also the worship of the holy mystery of God which is expressed in the liturgy. In this way, it will regain its splendor which is a reflection of the heavens and the glory of God, a foretaste of the heavenly Jerusalem and the heavenly liturgy (Heb 12:18–24). . . .

We can conclude that . . . God invites the world to take part in God's Being and yet remains transcendent vis-à-vis the world. God is not a part of the world. Consequently, the world is not divine; it is temporal. For this reason, there is a legitimate secularity. Yet, in sacred times, sacred places and sacred symbols, something shines forth in the midst of our temporal world; something opens up and is therefore fascinating. In them, God manifests God's self, communicates God's self but still does not become available, not materially objectified. . . .

We may not interpret our Christian existence either in liberal or purely existential terms. We have to learn once more to spell it out sacramentally so that we can see sacred places, sacred times and sacred symbols as icons that "present" something of the Holy without making it graspable. Therefore, we must not de-sacralize the liturgy, making it devoid of all of its splendor and the sublimity and fascination with the Holy. Liturgy is divine service, Holy Mass, we say. It is never just a communal celebration. Particularly in a leveling, secularized civilization which is widely void of meaning, the experience of the transcendence and the fascination of the Holy has a healing effect.

In this sense, we need what [Romano] Guardini already envisioned [in 1966]: not a reform of single rites, nor a reform of reform by replacing former reforms with different reforms. We cannot constantly mess with the liturgy. We need one, profound and comprehensive reform of our liturgical reforms, a renewed liturgical–sacramental culture, in which liturgy becomes epiphany; a liturgy that allows us to glimpse God's infinite glory and the immense fascination with the Holy in moments of silence, listening, adoration, and praise. —HEI, 20–26

MODERN SPIRITUAL MASTERS
Robert Ellsberg, Series Editor

This series introduces the essential writing and vision of some of the great spiritual teachers of our time. While many of these figures are rooted in long-established traditions of spirituality, others have charted new, untested paths. In each case, however, they have engaged in a spiritual journey shaped by the challenges and concerns of our age. Together with the saints and witnesses of previous centuries, these modern spiritual masters may serve as guides and companions to a new generation of seekers.

Already published:
Modern Spiritual Masters (edited by Robert Ellsberg)
Swami Abhishiktananda (edited by Shirley du Boulay)
Metropolitan Anthony of Sourozh (edited by Gillian Crow)
Eberhard Arnold (edited by Johann Christoph Arnold)
Pedro Arrupe (edited by Kevin F. Burke, S.J.)
Daniel Berrigan (edited by John Dear)
Thomas Berry (edited by Mary EvelynTucker and John Grim)
Dietrich Bonhoeffer (edited by Robert Coles)
Robert McAfee Brown (edited by Paul Crowley)
Dom Helder Camara (edited by Francis McDonagh)
Carlo Carretto (edited by Robert Ellsberg)
G. K. Chesterton (edited by William Griffin)
Joan Chittister (edited by Mary Lou Kownacki and Mary
    Hembrow Snyder)
Yves Congar (edited by Paul Lakeland)
The Dalai Lama (edited by Thomas A. Forsthoefel)
Alfred Delp, S.J. (introduction by Thomas Merton)
Catherine de Hueck Dogerty (edited by David Meconi, S.J.)
Virgilio Elizondo (edited by Timothy Matovina)
Jacques Ellul (edited by Jacob E. Van Vleet)
Ralph Waldo Emerson (edited by Jon M. Sweeney)
Charles de Foucauld (edited by Robert Ellsberg)
Mohandas Gandhi (edited by John Dear)
Bede Griffiths (edited by Thomas Matus)
Romano Guardini (edited by Robert A. Krieg)
Gustavo Gutiérrez (edited by Daniel G. Groody)
Thich Nhat Hanh (edited by Robert Ellsberg)

Abraham Joshua Heschel (edited by Susannah Heschel)
Etty Hillesum (edited by Annemarie S. Kidder)
Caryll Houselander (edited by Wendy M. Wright)
Pope John XXIII (edited by Jean Maalouf)
Rufus Jones (edited by Kerry Walters)
Clarence Jordan (edited by Joyce Hollyday)
Walter Kasper (edited by Patricia C. Bellm and Robert A. Krieg)
John Main (edited by Laurence Freeman)
Anthony de Mello (edited by William Dych, S.J.)
Thomas Merton (edited by Christine M. Bochen)
John Muir (edited by Tim Flinders)
John Henry Newman (edited by John T. Ford, C.S.C.)
Henri Nouwen (edited by Robert A. Jonas)
Flannery O'Connor (edited by Robert Ellsberg)
Karl Rahner (edited by Philip Endean)
Brother Roger of Taizé (edited by Marcello Fidanzio)
Oscar Romero (by Marie Dennis, Rennie Golden, and Scott Wright)
Albert Schweitzer (edited by James Brabazon)
Frank Sheed and Maisie Ward (edited by David Meconi)
Sadhu Sundar Singh (edited by Charles E. Moore)
Mother Maria Skobtsova (introduction by Jim Forest)
Dorothee Soelle (edited by Dianne L. Oliver)
Edith Stein (edited by John Sullivan, O.C.D.)
David Steindl-Rast (edited by Clare Hallward)
William Stringfellow (edited by Bill Wylie-Kellerman)
Pierre Teilhard de Chardin (edited by Ursula King)
Mother Teresa (edited by Jean Maalouf)
St. Thérèse of Lisieux (edited by Mary Frohlich)
Phyllis Tickle (edited by Jon M. Sweeney)
Henry David Thoreau (edited by Tim Flinders)
Howard Thurman (edited by Mary Krohlich)
Leo Tolstoy (edited by Charles E. Moore)
Evelyn Underhill (edited by Emilie Griffin)
Vincent Van Gogh (by Carol Berry)
Jean Vanier (edited by Carolyn Whitney-Brown)
Swami Vivekananda (edited by Victor M. Parachin)
Simone Weil (edited by Eric O. Springsted)
John Howard Yoder (edited by Paul Martens and Jenny Howells)